THE SOUTH'S
STRUGGLE

THE SOUTH'S STRUGGLE

AMERICA'S HOPE

WALTER DONALD KENNEDY

The South's Struggle: America's Hope
Copyright© 2022 Walter Donald Kennedy

ALL RIGHTS RESERVED. No part of this publication may be reproduced, distributed, or transmitted in any form or by any means, including photocopying, recording, or other electronic or mechanical methods, or by any information storage and retrieval system without the prior written permission of the publisher, except in the case of very brief quotations embodied in critical reviews and certain other noncommercial uses permitted by copyright law.

Produced in the Republic of South Carolina by

SHOTWELL PUBLISHING LLC
Post Office Box 2592
Columbia, So. Carolina 29202
www.ShotwellPublishing.com

ISBN 978-1-947660-68-7

FIRST EDITION

10 9 8 7 6 5 4 3 2 1

CONTENTS

INTRODUCTION i
THE SOUTH'S STRUGGLE: AMERICA'S HOPE

CHAPTER I 1
MAKE DIXIE GREAT AGAIN!

CHAPTER II 12
BATTALIONS: FORWARD INTO LINE MARCH!

CHAPTER III 19
CURRENT EVENTS AND SOUTHERN HISTORY

CHAPTER IV 25
THE FIGHTING SPIRIT

CHAPTER V 34
CONFEDERATE COUNTER-ATTACK

CHAPTER VI 40
THE SCORPION'S STING

CHAPTER VII 47
BETSY ROSS, THE RACIST?

CHAPTER VIII 53
YOUR YANKEE SHOT AND YOUR FREEDOM

CHAPTER IX..69
SCV: THE WELL-KEPT SECRET

CHAPTER X..75
ROBERT E. LEE: TRAITOR AND DEFENDER OF SLAVERY?

CHAPTER XI..84
ANTI-SOUTH BIGOTRY CONTINUES

CHAPTER XII...91
SCV AND FIGHTING HATE

CHAPTER XIII..95
MAKING HISTORY vs REGRETTING HISTORY

CHAPTER XIV..102
VICTORY: YES, WE CAN!

CHAPTER XV..111
THE STAB IN THE BACK

CHAPTER XVI..124
WHERE DO WE GO FROM HERE?

CHAPTER XVII...132
TOWARD THE LIBERATION OF SOUTHERN STATES

CHAPTER XVIII..141
THE HIGH-FLYING FLAG

CHAPTER XIX..156
VINDICATING DIXIE'S YOUNG WARRIORS

CHAPTER XX 176
SEE, WE TOLD Y'ALL SO!

CHAPTER XXI 184
THE THREE PHASES OF SOUTHER VICTORY

CHAPTER XXII..195
THE FORGOTTEN 11TH AMENDMENT

CHAPTER XXIII 208
THE LITTLE VERB THAT CAUSED A BIG WAR

CONCLUDING COMMENTS 218
AMERICA'S HOPE: ANOTHER TIME AND ANOTHER FORM

ABOUT THE AUTHOR..221

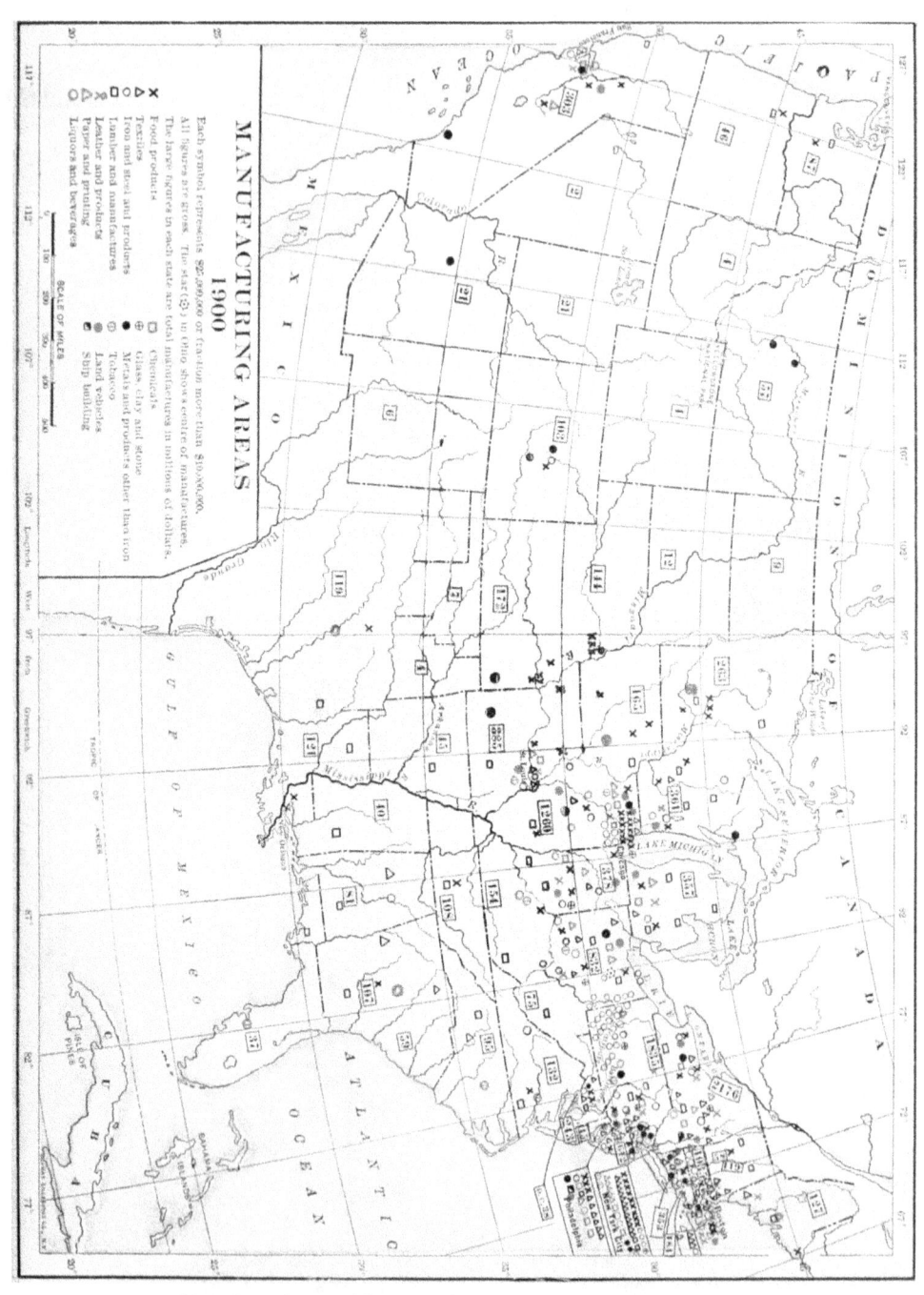

Manufacturing Map from Harper's Atlas of American History. Courtesy of loc.gov.

Introduction

THE SOUTH'S STRUGGLE: AMERICA'S HOPE

IN MODERN-DAY AMERICA it is politically incorrect to state the obvious fact of an individual's male or female status. Where once only males and females populated American society, in today's politically correct, woke America there is unlimited and unknowable amount of gender choices. Where once a man attempting to use a "female" restroom would have been arrested, today if one attempts to stop such action, such an attempt may very well find one attacked and/or arrested. In traditional America, communism, Marxism, and socialism were condemned and resisted but today's America embraces and promotes the most radical aspects of communism, Marxism, and socialism. In traditional America, the police were honored as public servants, in woke America police are demonized. In traditional America the Soviet Union was relentlessly condemned for closing churches and attacking Christians, in woke America closing churches and attacks upon Christians are now commonplace. The same evil, neo-Marxist force that is now destroying America began this process by attacking traditional Southern values. Before George Washington and Thomas Jefferson were attacked by neo-Marxists, Jefferson Davis and Robert E. Lee were attacked.

As pointed out by many in the Southern Rights movement, the attack upon the South was just a prelude to an attack upon all traditional American values. By assigning ignominious guilt and infamy to anyone or anything even remotely associated with slavery, the neo-Marxists were setting the stage for the final destruction of the United States flag and ultimately the Constitution. Remember, the thirteen stripes on the United States flag represent thirteen "slave-holding states." If one can condemn the Confederate flag because each star represents a slave-holding state, it is therefore only reasonable to condemn the United States flag—and as is noted in the following chapters, that is now being done. If one condemns the Confederate States of America because of slavery, what will be done to the Constitution of the United States which in three places recognizes, defines, and defends, slavery? A correct understanding of Southern history will destroy the neo-Marxist's falsehood about traditional American values. Thus, as it is stated herein, the South is "America's Hope."

From its founding in 1607 at Jamestown, Virginia, the South has been faced with many challenges. To the amazement of many, out of a vast wilderness, the South overcame many obstacles thereby creating a vibrant and prosperous society. Unfortunately, the truth about the first 254 years (1607-1861) of Southern success has been either under told or totally misrepresented by her perennial nemesis, the Yankee Empire. Most modern educated, more correctly modern indoctrinated, Americans have been raised upon the fable of the United States as "one nation indivisible" and have little knowledge about the nature of the great divide that was and to this day exists within these United States. America's Founding Fathers, such as John Adams of Massachusetts and Patrick Henry of Virginia, warned of the danger inherent in a union of people (Northerners and Southerners) so dissimilar. This North-South divide has never disappeared. The great American divide remains to this day and is displayed in how the victorious Yankee speaks of its defeated and occupied foe—the Confederate States of America.

Modern media, education, and other social information outlets all push the neo-Marxist, i.e., Yankee false narrative of a hate-filled, racist Southland. According to this false narrative, the South fought the "Civil War" in order to maintain the institution of slavery and after defeat, it was the South which sought to impose Jim Crow laws upon the re-united nation. This false narrative is an outgrowth of the deep North-South divide and is used to further the political and economic goals of the Yankee Empire. The post-War Yankee Empire was built upon a defeated people who were punished with poverty while the Yankee Empire experienced a golden "Gilded Age." A Gilded Age map of the United States displays where this post Appomattox prosperity and growth was taking place. The map demonstrates that the only place in the "re-united" United States of America that was not part of the Gilded Age was the defeated and occupied Confederate States of America. As the photo of this author's father and uncle, circa 1915, demonstrates, Southern poverty did not disappear with the end of Reconstruction. Even as late as 1948, this author's great aunt was being treated for Pellagra, a disease of malnutrition. Pellagra was unheard of in the South before Yankee invasion and occupation  but became a scourge (more like a Confederate States "pandemic") throughout the post-War South. Before Yankee invasion and occupation, the South was prosperous and a net exporter of food. After invasion and occupation, the South could not even feed her own people—as the Roman Empire noted of its conquered territory, vae victis, woe to the vanquished.

In the first 254 years of her existence, the South was able to overcome all obstacles with only one exception, the obstacle of the envious and hateful Yankee. Thus, when seeking to rid itself of the Yankee pestilence by recalling its delegated rights by the act of secession, the Yankee chose coercion via invasion, conquest, and occupation rather than allowing peaceful separation. It must be noted that according to the most fundamental document of American history, the Declaration of Independence, people in a free society have the unalienable right to "alter or abolish" any government they no longer desire to be associated with. Once the offending government has been abolished, the people have the unalienable right to "institute new Government...as to them shall seem most likely to effect their Safety and Happiness."

In total and complete disregard to the very words of the Declaration of Independence, the Yankee Empire, i.e., the United States of America, invaded, conquered, and has since that conquest held the former

Confederate States of America as a quasi-colony. Many Southerners question why the Yankee pushes their blatant false narrative about the War for Southern Independence and Southern history.

To understand why the Yankee acts in such a manner, one must understand two related truths: (1) the South (the Confederate States of America) is and continues to be a defeated and conquered nation; (2) to allow the truth about why the War for Southern Independence was fought and the truth about the denial to the Southern people of the American right to "alter or abolish" any government, would expose the Yankee Empire to the world as a colonial oppressor. Being thus exposed, said exposure could inspire within the defeated populace a desire for a remedy to their oppression.

At the end of the War for Southern Independence, General Lee warned the world that with the defeat of the South, the United States would become "aggressive abroad and despotic at home." With General Lee's warning in mind remember that the Yankee Empire clothes itself with several self-righteous labels such as "land of the free," "liberty and justice for all," "defender of democracy," and "seeking only good for foreign nations." The most fundamental document of these United States, the Declaration of Independence, proclaims that any people have the right to remove a government they no longer respect and establish another more to their liking. The core value and spirit of this document proclaims that "If you can't leave, you are not free." By denying the people of the Southern States the American Right to "alter or abolish" a distasteful government and establishing one more to their liking, the Yankee Empire trampled upon the very idea that America was the "land of the free." As the Gilded Age map, alluded to previously, points out, "liberty and justice for all" did not include the people of the conquered Confederate States of America. The "aggressive abroad" foreign policy which began with the invasion and conquest of the Confederate States of America was expanded to include the overturning of the constitutional monarchy of Hawaii; the forceful partitioning (secession) of Panama from Columbia; replacing the Spanish colonial power in the Philippines with the United States; and waging war upon the Philippine patriots who fought against both colonial powers, Spain and the United States. To the mortification of any knowledgeable American, these Philippine Patriots were fighting against colonialism just like America's Founding Fathers in 1776.

The "aggressive abroad" foreign policy of the Yankee Empire took the United States into China to secure for Yankee merchants their share of China's market place. These international interventions point out that Yankee foreign policy, just like the War to PREVENT Southern Independence, was pursued for the financial benefit of the Yankee Empire. Promoting democracy or the uplifting of foreign people was never the central purpose of the Yankee's "aggressive abroad" foreign policy—General Lee was right; the Confederacy was just the first of many conquered and exploited nations!

For at least 75 years after the War for Southern Independence the vast majority of Southerners understood the correctness of the Cause of the South. Thus, numerous monuments and memorial holidays were established and celebrated throughout the South. During this time an unspoken (tacit) agreement or bargain existed between the defeated and the victor. This tacit agreement allowed the South to honor its Confederate Veterans and have all "Civil War" veterans recognized as honorable Americans fighting for "what they believed to be correct." As long as the South remained loyal to the new order, that is, the new indivisible Union controlled by Northern interests and did not seek secession, Southern heroes would be treated as American heroes and the South would also be allowed nominal control of their state governments. The South has fully upheld it's part of this tacit agreement (bargain), as the white crosses of thousands of Southern dead on foreign battlefields testify. Descendants of Confederate Veterans rose to some of the highest ranks in the United States military. During WWII the highest-ranking American officer to be killed in action was General Simon Bolivar Buckner Jr. the son of Confederate General Simon Bolivar Buckner. During that same war, the highest-ranking Naval officer, Admiral Chester Nimitz, was the grandson of a Confederate officer. From WWI through the Cold War, the United States Army's 31st Infantry Division, The Dixie Division, proudly displayed the Confederate Flag and otherwise paid homage to its Confederate lineage.

In spite of the South's unwavering loyalty to the new Union, the Yankee Empire has completely broken the North/South bargain. It must be emphasized that the South, up to now, has kept its part of the bargain. The bargain was broken by the Yankee Empire and its neo-Marxist sycophants. One has only to look at the removal of all things Confederate from United States Military bases and the desecration of and/or removal of Confederate monuments from public display to prove the truth of this statement—the bargain is broken. As Daniel Webster once noted, "A bargain broken on one side is broken on all sides."

Where once the majority of Americans in the North and a super majority in the South, honored Confederate Veterans and respected the South, today all things Confederate and most things Southern are ridiculed, condemned, and banished from society. Two quick examples will demonstrate how insidious and complete this process has been. While watching a History Channel program on the development of the hand-gun in America, the history "expert" noted that the cap and ball revolver was "used in the Civil War when the South was fighting to keep slavery alive." On another program explaining the history of the States of the United States, when talking about a Southern State, slavery was always a major item to be discussed. Yet, when talking about Northern States, especially New England States, very little or nothing was said about the nefarious African slave trade nor the huge profits made by Yankee bankers and businesses suppling goods to Southern plantations. The South's making money from cotton produced by slave labor is always regarded as evil but the North's making money from that same cotton produced by slave labor is never condemned. Multiply these two false narratives by thousands in the media, education, political, and religious institutions and one can begin to understand why Americans in general and Southerners in particular are abandoning the Cause of the South—thus, we must "take back the narrative."

The more favorable view of the South that existed 75 years ago no longer exists. The "narrative" about Southern history and patriotism has been turned upside down in modern "progressive" America. Understanding the reality of modern-day anti-South bigotry compelled Paul Gramling, Jr., who in 2017, was the Lt. Commander-in-Chief of the Sons of Confederate Veterans, to approach the Kennedy Twins with a challenge. Gramling foresaw the need of establishing a new system within the SCV to "take back the narrative." The central theme of this effort was informing the general public of the truth about Southern history and why they should be proud to be Southerners. Observing several years of failed efforts of protecting Confederate monuments and memorials via law suits and appeals for fairness from the political establishment, it was obvious that doing the same thing over and over was a losing strategy. A new strategy looking toward final victory over our neo-Marxist enemies was needed. It was determined that the SCV must embrace new and different tactics in order to realize the strategic goal of final victory. As explained in chapter XXI, this effort would consist of three phases. The first phase in which the SCV must take the lead, consists of "educating" the general public on the correct view of Southern heritage and history. Following that effort, more direct political action leading to ultimate victory must be pursued. Commander-in-Chief Gramling desired the establishment of a new system within the SCV to "take back the narrative." As noted, the central theme of this effort was informing the general public about the truth of Southern history and why they should be proud to be Southerners. Therefore, a strategy for final victory by embracing new and different tactics was launched—the Southern Victory Campaign. This campaign consisted of the formation of the Confederate Legion, a new website, Make Dixie Great Again, and efforts to entice SCV camps and members to push this effort to final victory.

The Sons of Confederate Veterans have been exceptionally good at preforming tasks such as genealogy research, cleaning and protecting graves of Confederate Veterans, dedicating new Confederate monuments and raising giant Confederate flags. Because the truth about Southern history was common knowledge fifty years ago, such efforts were all that was needed to, in the words of General Stephen D. Lee, "vindicate the Cause for which they fought." But today, the truth of Southern history is no longer common knowledge. Rather, there is a multitude of anti-South bigots striving to indoctrinate Americans in general and Southerners in particular with a neo-Marxist false narrative—thus we need to "take back the narrative." The simple fact is if we do not tell the truth about the South, only the hate-filled anti-South neo-Marxist version will be heard. This was not the case fifty years ago but it is today's new reality.

The Sons of Confederate Veterans (SCV) and other Southern Rights activists must learn how to fight this 21st century enemy with the weapons and tools appropriate for this time and this struggle. Cleaning a Confederate Veteran's gravesite in praiseworthy but a clean grave cannot tell anyone what that veteran was fighting to secure; erecting new Confederate memorials and monuments is laudable but monuments do not speak, they cannot tell the world what they are memorializing; raising a giant Confederate flag is awe inspiring but that flag cannot tell a non-informed public what it represents. Who then will tell the story or speak for our veterans if not us? The answer is both simple and frightening. If we don't provide the public with correct information (take back the narrative), neo-Marxist enemies of the South will provide their hate-filled narrative.

In an effort to defeat the South's 21st century enemies, the SCV initiated the Southern Victory Campaign. Not only would the SCV challenge the neo-Marxist narrative but the total defeat of the South's enemies is the ultimate goal (as will be explained in 'Victory: Phase I, II, & III,' chapter XXI). But how can this be done? By coming to an understanding that this 21st century battle is in large part a public relations battle, the SCV established the Confederate Legion (CL). Ninety per cent of money raised via membership dues and donations to the CL is dedicated to placing before the general public positive information about the South and the SCV. The SCV has never had such a strategic "marketing" plan. As stated in chapter IX, the SCV has been a well-kept secret. Making the general public of the South aware of what the SCV is all about and why Southerners should be proud of their Southern heritage is foundational to ultimate victory. To do this several tools have been created for use by SCV camps such as: (1) pro-South videos, (2) radio ads that promote the Southern view and the SCV, (3) sample letters to be sent to local civic organizations, leaders, and politicians, (4) Southern Defenders, colorful hand-outs to be given away at festivals, gun shows, living histories, which promote a positive view of the South and the SCV, (5) Confederate Counter Attacks, every two months a new pro-South theme is pushed by the CL with appropriates ads, videos, and sample letters which camps are encouraged to participate in, (6) encouraging camps and SCV members to use various social media outlets to promote this effort. These tools, radio ads, videos, letters, and articles are displayed on the new SCV website, Make Dixie Great Again. This type of robust (radical) public outreach is something never tried by the SCV. But if we seek total victory for the Cause of the South, Southerners must get our message before the general public.

Part of the responsibility of the Chief of Heritage Operations of the SCV is to produce an article published in the Confederate Veteran magazine: 'Forward the Colors.' The following chapters will include the first 20 'Forward the Colors' articles published during my terms as Chief of Heritage Operations. At the end of most chapters there will be an additional article that supports the emphasis of the original 'Forward the Colors' article. Chapter XXI 'Three Phases to Victory' is written by Ron Kennedy, author of *Dixie Rising: Rules for Rebels*. Chapter XXI offers a short overview of the Kennedy Twins' suggestions for how total victory can be achieved. Every chapter is intended to support the effort to "take back the narrative."

The strategic goal of the Southern Victory Campaign is to engage the South's neo-Marxist enemy in the public forum in such a manner as to assure that Southerners, and hopefully all Americans, will reject the neo-Marxist false narrative about the South and Traditional American Values. The use of these "tools" by SCV camps and members is designed to educate, motivate, and activate Southerners and thereby defeat the enemies of the South. We use education to inform the public, which will motivate the public and thereby, make people aware of the truth of Southern history/heritage at which point many will become activists. Activists will be eager to join us in our struggle both in the defense of Southern heritage and Traditional American Values, as well as in the political arena where those who stab us in the back (see chapter 15) are defeated and OUR people are elected.

Today, the SCV has over 800 camps (local organizations). If every camp would embrace the methods described herein, the SCV would no longer be a "Well Kept Secret" (see chapter 9). Not only would the general public understand who we are and why we love the South, but most importantly, the political establishment will take notice. They would then understand (fear) that they have a vocal, well-organized group to contend with if they trample upon Southern history, heritage, and rights. As repeatedly stated in the following chapters, WE CAN WIN! But we will not win by doing the same things we were doing 50 years ago. This is a 21st century fight and we must use 21st century tactics and weapons to defeat our enemy.

Chapter I

MAKE DIXIE GREAT AGAIN!

THERE IS AN OLD STORY about a tranquil town on the edge of a beautiful and peaceful river. One day town folks saw a man who had fallen in the river and was going under for the last time. Volunteers rushed out in boats and saved the man. Over the years more and more drowning people were pulled out of the once peaceful river. At last, the volunteers were overwhelmed and were losing more victims than they were saving. At a town meeting they were discussing raising money to hire a fulltime rescue squad when an old man stood up and declared that the money would not be sufficient! "Why not," he was asked? Because, explained the wise old man, the river can drown more people than we can save. His suggestion was to go up river and find out what was causing people to fall in the river and fix that problem. The town folk had been **reactive** instead of being **proactive**—they were engaging in what is known as "downstream thinking" when the problem called for "upstream thinking." For Southerners, it's time to go "upstream" and fix the problem!

Our monuments, flags, and Southern heritage activities were not removed or banned by the NAACP, ANTIFA, or the liberal mainline media—they were removed or banned by elected Southern politicians. These politicians have no reason to fear a negative reaction from Southerners who supported keeping monuments, flags and positive Southern heritage activities—such as Confederate units marching in parades. Opinion polls have demonstrated that up to 70% of Southerners desire to keep our Confederate monuments—a substantial number of black Southerners help to make up that 70%! Our failure has been that we have not **mobilized** the 70% plus of our fellow Southerners who agree with us! Our monuments were removed by judges, mayors, councilmen, representatives, and governors who must stand for re-election or in many cases face the possibility of a recall petition! The pressure group that makes the most noise causes the most re-election fear for politicians—our enemy has the ability to create "noise" via a friendly media and educational establishment. It is time for the SCV to counter their "noise" with an aroused public that supports Southern heritage—it is time to publicly vindicate the Cause!

Your new Commander-in-Chief and Chairman of Heritage Operations are planning to establish a South-wide educational public-relations (PR) campaign—in other words, "we are going upstream" and fight the real battle. As Commander Gramling explained at our recent Reunion, we are going on the offensive with our 'Southern Victory Campaign.' This effort will arouse the 70% passive supporters of Southern heritage and turn them into **active** Southern heritage supporters—active supporters, who will be eager to join us and demand that their elected officials give fair, balanced, and equal treatment to Southern heritage. The first step of this effort is the establishment of the Confederate Legion (CL) which will fund a **REAL** Confederate counter-offensive. The Confederate Legion will fund positive, pro-South ads to be run via Radio Free Dixie (RFD) which will be the center piece of the PR effort; second, we will identify fair and/or friendly media outlets (Confederate Media List) and start working with them to promote our Cause; and third, upgrade and network our existing social media outlets from the national level to the camp level.

The Confederate Legion will be the ramrod for this new (actually first-time) SCV counter-offensive. To kick off this "going on the offensive" effort we will need 1,000 people in each Army to sign-up to the CL by donating $50 a year. *Fifty dollars a year is less than the price of four Cokes a month for a year.* We can and must do this if we are going to "vindicate the Cause of the South." Funds raised by the CL will be used to buy pro-South ads on Country and Talk radio stations across the Confederation. Ninety cents out of every dollar raised by the CL will be spent on ads promoting a positive view of the South. The remaining ten cents of each dollar raised will be used to defer CL operation costs.

Think about having hundreds of positive one or two-minute, pro-South ads aired on radio stations across the South. Imagine the impact such pro-South information will have on the general public—a public that already passively supports Southern heritage. Remember, most people do not understand the true history of the South nor do they understand the true value of our Southern heritage. At last, we can begin to change that false narrative and replace it with the truth. In addition to the ads run by the CL, we will make all ads available to SCV camps and will encourage camps to run these ads on their local stations. At least four times a year the CL will promote special events via RFD such as 'Confederate Diversity Month' in February, 'Great Revival in the Confederate Army' during month of Easter, 'America's Secession Holiday' in July, and 'America's First Thanksgiving' in November. We, the members of the Sons of Confederate Veterans, understand the truth but our neighbors seldom hear the truth. If we fail to tell our neighbors the truth about the South, the only version of Southern history they will ever hear is the victor's biased and distorted view of our Confederate ancestors and their Cause. These radio ads will not only educate people but will also direct the audience to our SCV Heritage Defense web site, "Make Dixie Great Again" (www.makedixiegreatagain.org). This website will provide links to our YouTube channel, videos on various Southern issues, selected articles from the Confederate Veteran, and other positive information about the South as well as SCV membership information.

Radio Free Dixie will commence airing ads when we have 1,000 CL supporters in each Army but our goal is to ultimately have at least *three* to *five* thousand CL members in each army—at that time the SCV will become a common household name across the South! This pro-South public relations counter-offensive will be a major part of the SCV's recruitment and retention effort. This effort can be the turning point in the war against the South and you can be one of the founding Southern Patriots making it happen. Information on how to join the Confederate Legion will be available in the November-December 2018 issue of the *Confederate Veteran*.

Several months ago, Commander Gramling instructed the Kennedy Twins to start working on his Southern Victory Campaign. To that point we have for the past three months been working to secure domain names, web pages, video and audio capability. For the past four months names of friendly (or at least fair) media outlets have been compiled and added to the Confederate Media List. Here is how you can help us and be a part of Commander Gramling's Southern Victory Campaign. We need to identify fair and/or friendly radio, T.V., and print media outlets across the South. This collected information will be used to promote our efforts in a friendlier market place than we normally deal with. Help us identify these media outlets by forwarding to WDKennedy@Reagan.com the following information on "fair and/or friendly media":

> For radio or TV stations: call letters, U.S. mailing address, e-mail address, fax number, phone number and name of host;

> For newspapers: name, U.S. mailing address, e-mail address, phone number, fax number and name/e-mail address of friendly/fair editor or columnist.

This info is crucial for getting started with Radio Free Dixie. Remember, only you can prevent the destruction of Dixie. Only you can assure that the **vindication** of our Confederate ancestors and the Cause of the South will become a reality. Remember, only you can MAKE THE SOUTH GREAT AGAIN! If we fail at this, we and our beloved Southland will be forever consigned to infamy. Southerners, it's time for "upstream thinking and action. It's time to march to the sound of battle. Let us **Make the South Great Again!**

THE SOUTH'S STOCKHOLM SYNDROME

The following article will explain why so many Southerners seem to have embraced or at least quietly tolerate the Yankee Empire's false narrative about the South both as it relates to the War for Southern Independence and race relations in America.

 The Stockholm Syndrome is a condition where captives or hostages develop a psychological attachment and loyalty to their captors. Psychologists often describe this syndrome as a "survival strategy." This strategy is employed by captives when all hope for returning to a normal life appears to be lost. By befriending one's all-powerful captors, life is preserved within the new "normal" order. This syndrome was first described in 1973 following a hostage standoff in Stockholm, Sweden. Several hostages were held for six days in a bank vault, tortured, and tormented by their captor. Upon being released, none of the hostages would testify against their captor and even worked in the legal defense of their former captor. For Americans the most noted case of the Stockholm Syndrome centers around the 1974 kidnapping of Patty Hearst, a member of the wealthy and prominent Hearst Family of California. Miss Hearst was kidnapped by leftist terrorists known as the Symbionese Liberation Army (SLA). Hearst's subsequent cooperation with the SLA, including armed robbery of a bank, resulted in her arrest for bank robbery.

 In most cases only a few people are afflicted with this syndrome. But at times and especially under stressful political conditions large segments of a society, and even nations, can suffer from symptoms of the Stockholm Syndrome. In fictional literature this syndrome is demonstrated in such works as Orwell's *1984* or Huxley's *Brave New World*. In real life it can be seen in any nation that has been conquered and occupied by an all-powerful aggressor. For example, with the fall of France in 1940, a pro-German rogue republic, the Vichy Republic, was established in what was known as the "free zone" in France. An attitude of "go along to get along" was soon adopted and followed by many Frenchmen. This attitude resulted in the citizens of the conquered nation becoming "loyal" to the Nazi invaders of France. This quasi loyalty was displayed by the French in their cooperation with the Nazi's efforts to arrest Jews and partisan (loyal) French patriots, assisting in Nazi war production, and allowing, without protest, the romantic relationship between French women and Nazi soldiers.

During the Cold War the people of nations occupied by the Soviet Union soon began "doing business" with their occupiers to the point that the defeated and occupied nations of Eastern Europe played a large part in the defense of the Soviet Union. In 1956 the Warsaw Pact was established whereby Eastern European nations "invited" troops from the Soviet Union to be stationed in their country to defend them from Western aggression. Not only did Eastern European nations "invite" foreign Soviet troops into their country but each occupied nation's military provided support to the Soviet Union as member nations of the Warsaw Pact. As Irish Confederate General Patrick Cleburne and other Irishmen learned in 1846, when your country is defeated and you are faced with starvation, service in the occupying nation's military may be the only thing that prevents starvation. This is something conquerors use to fill the ranks of the empires' foreign military—the very military used to occupy the defeated nation.

This rationalizing of the relationship between the conquered and the conquerors to the point where it leads to the voluntary cooperation with the former enemy is nothing less than a societal form of the Stockholm Syndrome. These examples demonstrate how and why people can and will rationalize their action vis-à-vis their onetime enemy and present-day captors.

Empires are also eager to employ false respect for their conquered masses as a means of promoting the empire's safety. For example, the Soviet Union's Warsaw Pact was named for the capital of Poland. Polish history abounds with stories of wars and struggles with Russia. One would think that Warsaw, Poland, would not be the seat of power for the Soviet Union's Eastern European defensive organization; after all, Poland and Russia fought at least fourteen wars between 1558 and 1939. The Soviet conquerors of Eastern Europe understood how to use false flattery to insure the loyalty of their subjected people. Also, just as the French had learned in 1939 and the Irish in 1846, Poland and Eastern Europe learned in 1955; a conquered people usually will do those things necessary to rationalize the embracing of their conquering master. This "rationalizing" of the new relationship between themselves and their oppressor tends to hide and sugarcoat past and present sufferings of their people. What is true for the preceding nations and people is also true for the people of the conquered and occupied Confederate States of America.

The very fact that most Southerners do not accept nor remotely understand the depth of their second-class status in the United States demonstrates the effectiveness of 150 years of Yankee propaganda. Since the defeat and occupation of the Confederate States of America the Yankee Empire has used "education" to brainwash each generation of Southerners primarily by teaching four false narratives:

(1) we are all better off since the South lost the war;

(2) All Americans have equal access to a high standard of living;

(3) equality before the law is foundational to "our way of life"; and,

(4) the "Civil War" is over and only extremists would view the fight for Southern freedom as worthy of a contemporary endeavor.

The embracing of these false narratives by the people of the South is clearly driven home in a recently released book dealing with a distinguished Louisiana Confederate unit. The author, a well-respected history professor, did an excellent job chronicling the heroic and tenacious military élan of some of the Confederacy's most outstanding warriors in the cause of Southern independence. Nevertheless, on the last page of his otherwise outstanding book, he proceeds to inform his readers that "The Civil War is Really Over." To support his contention that the "Civil War" is over, the author details how the Louisiana National Guard (the descendants of the Louisiana Tigers) and the New York National Guard (which traces its history back to the Irish Brigade—both units being "Civil War" units) were combined and fought side by side in Iraq. The last time these two units were "together" was during the Battle of Malvern Hill when the Louisianans and their fellow Confederates were trying to expel an invader from their country. Yes, the military actions of the War for Southern Independence are over, but does that mean that the young men from Louisiana and the young men from New York live in a land of freedom and equal opportunity? If indeed the so-called war is over then these "brothers-in-arms" should have a lifestyle that is equal and free—freedom as given to us by our colonial ancestors. Remember that the foundation of American freedom is announced in the Declaration of Independence. In that document our ancestors boldly proclaimed that legitimate government only existed by the *consent* of the governed. When *coercion* replaces *consent*, freedom is nullified and an illegitimate government replaces the once legitimate government. It is upon these points that the author's fantasy of "one nation united, equal and free" begins to disintegrate.

One cannot compare but must contrast the pathetic emotional appeal of this Louisiana author/professor's statement to the words of Louisiana's Governor, Sam H. Jones, who in 1943 stated, "But here in America, for more than a hundred years, we have witnessed and lived through...a process that has for its purpose the reduction of the fairest portion of our country to the permanent status of a *conquered province*. For more than a hundred years the Southern part of the United States has been the victim of a studied plan to overcome its [the South] superior economic advantages and reduce it [the South] to a state of *economic vassalage*." [Emphasis added] Men who are citizens of a "conquered province" and who have been reduced to "economic vassalage" are the inferiors not the equals of their conquerors who, flushed with ill-gotten gain (filthy lucre), have become wealthy at the expense of the conquered.

Speaking in 1943, during the middle of WWII, Governor Jones condemned the plundering of the South not just during the War for Southern Independence but every year since the defeat and occupation of the once free and prosperous South. This plundering has reduced the South from the most prosperous region of the nation to the nation's poorest region. As Governor Jones noted, "So in spite of the fact that we have today the same land, the same climate, the same natural resources, the same geographical position—and the same strains of blood in our citizenship, 97.8 percent of which is native born—we have the lowest income, the least wealth, the poorest educational facilities, the least number of books in circulation, the smallest bank deposits, the smallest percentage of insurance assets, the most limited advantages in health and hygiene, the most eroded soils, the poorest agriculture and the most ineffective representation in the affairs of the nation; not because of the quality of that leadership but because of the existing political system." So, professor, where is the "one nation with liberty and justice for all" where the children of the South have an equal chance for education, professional advancement, and equal pay? That nation does not exist! What does exist is a commercial empire controlled by Wall Street in New York and K Street in Washington. This empire is more than willing to use Southern children as cannon fodder for their no-win wars to protect their commercial empire. As General Smedley Butler, USMC, the most decorated Marine during his lifetime, noted in his book *War is a Racket,* the American commercial empire has turned the American military into Wall Street hit men.

As pointed out in *Punished with Poverty: The Suffering South,* the reduction of the South from the wealthiest section of the United States to the most poverty laden section is no accident. In 1943, Gov. Jones noted that at one time the South was wealthy well beyond the imagination of modern-day Southerners. More recently a study from the University of California-Davis and Harvard University also "discovered" that indeed from the colonial era to 1860 the South was the wealthiest section of the United States. This wealth did not just reside on the large plantations but extended to free laborers of the South whose earnings were higher than Northern laborers. As Gov. Jones noted, "In the year 1850 the total wealth of the nation was approximately seven billion dollars of which 50 percent was located in the South. Today the total wealth is approximately 300 billion dollars of which the South has only 10 percent. In 1850 the South had better than 80 percent of the nation's exports; today it has only about 21 percent." How can any reasonable person, let alone a "professor," believe that the citizens of the defeated, conquered and occupied Confederate States of America live in a nation where, "The Civil War is Really Over." Those suffering the symptoms of the Stockholm Syndrome could hold and express such feelings but that does not change the dreadful fact of the ongoing poverty and social stigmatization associated with being a member of the defeated and occupied section of the empire. Not only was this impoverishment true in 1943, when Governor Jones was speaking but today Southerners are still second-class Americans, subjects of the Yankee Empire, and citizens of the defeated and occupied captive nation, the Confederate States of America.

In 1943 Governor Jones of Louisiana was merely exposing for all to see the consequences and reality of defeat for the South. During the War for Southern Independence a leading Northern newspaper clearly stated its desire to extract a terrible retribution from the South: "We mean to *conquer* them, *Subjugate* them" and never permit Southerners to "return to peaceful and contented homes...they must find *poverty* at their firesides, and see privation in the anxious eyes of mothers and the *rags of children*." This poverty lasted well beyond the War and Reconstruction—it continues to this day. This punishment of poverty is clearly demonstrated when looking at the U.S. median household income by state. Looking at median household income it is obvious that every Southern State falls *below* the national median household income—the War is Not over!

Today a child born in the South has a 30% lower-lifetime-income earning expectation than a child born in the North—the War is NOT over! The major institutions of learning, those institutions which fill the highest ranks of business, industry, and national political leadership are all located in the North and filled with Northern students—the War is NOT over! There are key cultural differences between Northern society and Southern society. For example: Southerners have the highest church attendance rate in the nation while the North has the lowest church attendance rate; the South has the highest per-capita charitable-giving rate while the North has the lowest per-capita charitable-giving rate; the lowest per-capita income is found in Southern States, while the highest per-capita income is found in Northern States; Southern States have the highest conservative voting record in the nation while their Northern counterpart have the highest *liberal* voting record (this is a disaster for the South because in the U. S. Congress, liberals out vote Southern conservatives). NO, THE WAR IS NOT OVER—The South's Struggle continues!

Today it is the South and its cultural heritage that is under attack by the politically correct establishment. Everything from displaying the Ten Commandments to maintaining Confederate monuments is attacked, thus depriving a conquered people the right to display pride in their history, their spiritual values, their region, and their people. Despite all of this, we are assured that "The War is Really Over!" Here is the harsh truth that too many Southerners including Southern authors, professors, and political leaders do not want to hear: The false narrative that "The War is Really Over" is merely code-words for the sad reality of *Vae Victis*,

Woe to the Vanquished! For much too long the condition of social, economic and political poverty has been tolerated by the Southern people. This tolerance has been used by our conqueror to teach Southerners to accept their role as second-class Americans. This tolerance assures that Southerners will continue living under a government by *coercion* rather than demanding the American Right to live under a government by the free and unfettered *consent* of the governed. America's Founding Fathers understood that living under a government by coercion nullifies freedom—yet pacified Southerners pretend they can't see this reality. By ignoring this reality, we only assure that the next generation of Southerners, like the present one, will not be free. As citizens of the vanquished nation, the Confederate States of America, we can only ask, "How many years can some people exist before they are allowed to be free? How many times can a man turn his head and pretend he just does not see? The answer, my friend, is blowing in the wind."

THE ANSWER IS BLOWING IN THE WIND!

Chapter II

BATTALIONS:
FORWARD INTO LINE MARCH!

MY CONGRATULATIONS, ENCOURAGEMENT, and support to our fellow Confederates in North Carolina who are working day and night to secure justice for Silent Sam. This type of attack has become almost routine but this time around something is changing in our response. The neo-Marxist mob that pulled down Silent Sam has re-invigorated many otherwise silent Southerners. Our kith and kin across the South who detest the ongoing vulgar attacks against our Southern heritage, the South's Bible-Belt and conservative traditions are beginning to react against the vulgar mobs. But the most important change is how the SCV is preparing to answer these attacks. Commander Gramling's 'Southern Victory Campaign' will soon have in place the tools that will allow us to monitor and answer our critics but, **and this is of the utmost importance**, we will begin the long-term effort to convert passive supporters into active supporters. When in the midst of battle, it is sometimes hard to realize that despite the turmoil immediately around, there is good news all along the battle line—good news that will eventually lead to wining the final victory—yes, I said FINAL VICTORY!

Here is some good news: In a recent poll conducted by Television Station WKRN in Nashville, Tennessee, 84% of the over 10,000 respondents expressed their desire to maintain Confederate monuments and memorials in their current location. This unscientific public opinion poll is similar to the scientific poll conducted in 2016 in Louisiana in which 88% of white and 47% of black Louisiana citizens expressed a desire to protect and maintain Confederate monuments. Even a liberal/progressive news service, CNN, was shocked when it did a survey of Americans, not just Southerners, and found that 57% of those surveyed favor maintaining Confederate monuments. These surveys demonstrate that the vast majority of Americans and especially Southerners agree with us and not with the NAACP, ANTIFA or other neo-Marxist groups. We have a vast and enormous pool of inactive or passive public support for maintaining Southern heritage. Our problem is not that we do not have public support but our problem is that we have failed to tap into this vast reservoir of passive support. The Southern Victory Campaign is aimed at this vast reservoir of passive support and converting passive supporters into active supporters. The growth of SCV membership will parallel the growth of the pool of active Southern heritage supporters.

The big question is "How do we convert passive supporters into active supporters?" First, the easy thing to do: We must learn to toot our own horn. There is an old saying that if you do not toot your own horn, said horn shall go un-tooted. Thanks to past leaders, the SCV has been very active in some great civic functions such as: (1) Numerus giant Confederate Flags posted on well-traveled highways, (2) New Confederate monuments placed and dedicated (more have gone up than have come down), (3) Strong support for Confederate Flag Day, (4) Confederation-wide Law Enforcement Appreciation Day, (5) Brooks Post-Graduate Medical Research grants (how many lives are positively impacted due to medical research funded by the SCV?), (6) Stand Watie Scholarship awards, (7) SCV support for the Sam Davis Christian Youth Camps, and many other similar activities. But here is a major problem we have allowed to develop: Many SCV members and the overwhelming majority of the general public are unaware of the SCV's numerous civic activities. In other words, our wonderful work for our community generally goes unheralded. We can do better and we must do better in letting our membership and the general public know what we are doing. In the September/October issue of the *Confederate Veteran,* I asked our members to forward to me the names and contact information of friendly and/or fair media outlets. In Louisiana alone, there are at least ten conservative talk-radio stations and 20 local, weekly friendly/fair newspapers. The big mainline news media will rarely run our news releases and if they do, they will use two lines of negative reporting for every positive line they give us. By going to these conservative stations and local papers, we can get our message to John Q. Public, i.e., our people. The next time a giant Flag goes up, we will let the world know about it or the next time a Brooks medical research grant is given to (let's say) fight childhood leukemia, the world will know what the SCV is doing! If Louisiana is typical, then there should be at least 450 fair/friendly media outlets in the 15 Southern States plus additional media from Divisions outside of Dixie. It's the job of our members to get us this information.

Our efforts with Radio Free Dixie (radio ads) and targeted internet ads will help us convert passive supporters into active supporters. Active supporters can and will use their voice and their votes to inform elected officials, who now quake before the neo-Marxist rabble, that it is time to stand firm and "do your duty or else!" It is time to make weak-kneed elected officials quake before an aroused, Southern populace. We must always remember that Confederate monuments that were removed or Confederate flags that were excluded from civic events were removed or excluded by weak-kneed elected officials. Furthermore, Confederate monuments that have been vandalized and destroyed by neo-Marxist mobs were vandalized while weak-kneed, "quaking" elected officials stood idly by. An activated Southern population will cause these "quaking, elected officials" to fear us (we vote in their elections; we are not an outside rent-a-mob) more than our politicians fear the neo-Marxist rabble.

We are in the process [2018] of building our new web site, Make Dixie Great Again, and believe it should be up and running by the first week in November, Visit us and support the Confederate Legion at: www.makedixiegreatagain.org

It is time, my fellow Southerners, to catch the spirit of the *La Marseillaise:*

Let's go! Children of the Nation!

The day of glory has arrived!

Against us stands tyranny

The bloody standard is raised!

To arms, Citizens!

Form your battalions!

Let's march,

Let's march!

TO ARMS, CITIZENS!

Walter D. (Donnie) Kennedy, Chief of Heritage Operations.

CHRISTIANS MARCHING WITH MARX

One of the main reasons the "Battalions" are not rushing forward in defense of our heritage is that so many ministers have bought into the so-called "Critical Race Theory." When Bible-Belt Christians are subjected to ministers who are promoting the neo-Marxist narrative, hope for forming the battalions decreases. Therefore, Americans in general and Southerners in particular, need to understand the dangers of religious leaders "marching with Marx."

In our modern age of political correctness, it is not uncommon to find various Christians, including many noted ministers and evangelists, snuggling up to the detractors of the South. In Mississippi during the fight to keep the Confederate flag emblem on its State flag, Mississippians heard "leading" ministers of various denominations condemn the so-called "hated symbol." In Georgia the same scenario was played out, only this time the preacher was in the Governor's chair and did all within his power to destroy any effort to protect the real flag of Georgia. In churches across the South the Fourth of July is celebrated with the shameful sounds of "The Battle Hymn of the Republic," but God protect anyone who requests the playing of "Dixie" in church.

Political Correctness has descended upon the South with a near fatal impact and all too often it is Christian leaders who are leading the assault. Warning the people of England about the lethal results of embracing Christian Socialism, Charles Spurgeon stated: "I would not have you exchange the gold of individual Christianity for the base metal of Christian Socialism." When one understands that virtually every radical socialist and communist in the United States at the time of the War for Southern Independence joined in the struggle against the South, the words of Spurgeon, a London Baptist minister, begin to have real meaning. The South had barely begun its struggle for independence when radical socialists, communists and even Karl Marx, began a war of words and of deeds against the cause of Southern independence. In an article written for *Die Presse*, a Vienna newspaper, Marx asserted that (1) the South was fighting to promote slavery, (2) the Confederate Constitution was a pro-slavery document, (3) Jefferson Davis was a Southern dictator, and (4) the United States Supreme Court was a willing tool of Southern slaveholders. The founders of modern-day communism, Karl Marx and Fredrick Engels, both served as Lincoln's unofficial European propaganda ministers during the War. Simply put, modern day, anti-South political correctness is an outgrowth of 19th century Marxist propaganda.

In an article written in late 2008, David Barton of Wall Builders fame and noted Evangelical Christian activist wrote an article excoriating and otherwise condemning the South for (1) defending slavery, (2) adopting a constitution that defended slavery, and (3) having leaders and a constitution that compelled states to accept slavery. While each of these charges can be easily debunked, what is so upsetting is to see an otherwise good Christian and defender of what he calls Constitutional government, embrace Marxist philosophy. And just for lagniappe, this Louisiana writer would like to know why Barton is attacking Southern heritage when he is the leader of an organization charged with defending Christian virtue and rights? According to more than one recent poll it is, and has been for a long time, the South that accords religion and the Bible the highest respect of any Americans. Why insult the people who are most likely to embrace the work of Wall Builders?

In 1894 Robert Ingersoll, a former Captain in the Illinois Cavalry, a radical Republican and a free thinker (the 19th century equivalent of today's secular humanists) gave an address in which he defended Lincoln's legacy as a free thinker. Ingersoll made a telling statement about why the so-called Civil War was fought: "The great stumbling block the great obstruction in Lincoln's way and in the way of thousands, was the old doctrine of State's Rights." Removing this "stumbling block" to the growth of big government was the very reason that none other than Adolf Hitler heaped praise upon Lincoln's action during the War for Southern Independence. Hitler also had to remove the last vestiges of what he called "Statal Rights" before he could establish his "perpetual and supreme" Reich. Marx's philosophical twin, Fredrick Engels, told Joseph Weydemeyer, a fellow communist, future leader in the Republican Party, and future Union General, that by forging one large and "indivisible" republic instead of many small republics, they would establish the ground work for the communist movement. With the death of real States' Rights everything that the advocates of big government desired became not only possible but also inevitable. Today nationalized banking is a reality; abortion on demand in any State is a reality; the removal of the Ten Commandments from a State building by Federal authorities is a reality. All of this happened because real States' Rights was destroyed by Lincoln's war—a war fought not to end slavery but to end REAL States' Rights. This is reality in modern America. This modern American reality was praised by Hitler and made possible by Lincoln, Marx, Engels and a host of other free thinkers. Marching with Lincoln and Marx is tantamount to exchanging the gold of constitutionally-limited government for the base metal of Federal empire.

Chapter III

CURRENT EVENTS AND SOUTHERN HISTORY

VIEWING CURRENT EVENTS is sometimes difficult for those of us who love our heritage as Americans and Southerners. The current neo-Marxist attack upon traditional American values is progressing like a tsunami of bigotry and hate. Yet there is good news out there and we need to be aware of some positive things that are happening today that are making our job as Southern patriots easier.

In November of 1989 the Berlin Wall came crashing down and with it the demise of the once mighty *perpetual and indivisible* union of the communist empire. What happened next made the secession of thirteen states from the Federal Union in 1861 appear logical and reasonable. The Union of the Soviet Socialist Republics (USSR) simply fell apart as the republics which had been invaded, conquered, and dominated by the central government in Russia began seceding from the once *perpetual* union. In the following years it seemed as if secession was breaking out all around the world. In 1994 the Kennedy Twins in *The South Was Right!* noted this process taking place: "It looks as if world events have at last caught up with Southern history. For us die-hard Confederates, we feel as if God's vindication is just around the corner."

In the intervening thirty years we have witnessed more secession movements in Quebec, Scotland, Catalonia; and Great Britain voted to secede from the European Union. Here in the United States the Vermont Republic and the California secession movement, Calexit, are pushing for peaceful secession. In addition to these movements, it is not uncommon to hear news reports about reestablishing the independent Republic of Texas. At this point in time, it seems as if John C. Calhoun and Jefferson Davis' view of American Federalism is being revisited by many non-Southerners. With this momentum behind us, it will become easier for us to "vindicate the Cause for which they [Confederate Veterans] fought." This point should not be overlooked by Southern patriots. Remember, our enemy has always attempted to condemn the South by claiming that secession was merely an excuse for defending slavery and racism. Liberals and other leftists historically have refused to hear and accept our arguments about real American Federalism. That stance is now harder for neo-Marxists to maintain.

Recently, I had the pleasure of attending a conference sponsored by the Abbeville Institute on "The Revival of Secession and State Nullification." Seven lectures were given on this subject, four of which were given by non-Southerners. Each speaker made the point that "times are changing" in regard to the idea for which the South struggled in 1861. The most shocking and eye-opening lecture was given by Marcus Ruiz Evans, a liberal Hispanic advocate of California secession. Mr. Evans lecture was titled 'Why California Secession Can Strengthen Genuine Federalism in America.' His major point was that the left is beginning to understand that, yes, the South had every right to secede in 1861 and it was not being done to protect the institution of slavery. When liberals begin to talk like this, we should understand that indeed "things are beginning to change." Other non-Southern speakers also noted the need for REAL Federalism, AKA States' Rights which is not what we have today. Today States can only do that which the Federal Government approves, therefore, we have States' *Privileges* not States' *Rights*. The important thing for the SCV to take note of is the changing views of many Americans about the issues which drove the War for Southern Independence— the right of secession. In a 2018 Zogby poll, 68% of Americans were willing to consider secession of their state from the union. The word secession no longer is inextricably tied to racism and slavery—a good first step in our effort to "vindicate the Cause for which they fought." Two term Oklahoma state Representative Dan Fisher spoke on the subject of 'The Role of the Executive in Asserting State Sovereignty.' As Rep. Fisher noted the role of elected officials at the state level will be key to restoring true Federalism (which he insists includes the right of nullification) in the United States. He noted that if true Federalism is not restored, America will become too polarized to be governed as a free society.

For those living near the coast you learn that sometimes one must launch a boat when the tide is right or lose the opportunity to set sail. For us in the Sons of Confederate Veterans, the preceding accounts of the beginning of a change in attitude about American Federalism, that is, REAL States' Rights, represents a tide we must soon capture if we are to 'vindicate the Cause for which they fought.' Let me remind you that the Preamble of the SCV Constitution states that members of the SCV affirm their "Allegiance to the Constitution of the United States of America...[and] a strict construction of all sections conferring power upon the Federal Government and the implied and understood reservations to the States." This is a short definition of American Federalism. It was this from of government that our Colonial Forefathers gave us in 1776 and the very same thing that our Confederate Forefathers defended for us in 1861. Lincoln and his army of invaders were the true enemies of American Federalism (even if the Rush Limbaughs of America don't understand this), our Confederate Forefathers were the defenders of Federalism and therefore defenders of the Constitution.

At last, we of the Sons of Confederate Veterans have tools ready to be used to "vindicate the Cause" of our forefathers. If you have not already visited our web site, Make Dixie Great Again, (www.makedixiegreatagain.org), please do so. If you have not joined in this pro-active effort of putting our message before our neighbors in Dixie, do so by going to Make Dixie Great Again, clicking on the Confederate Legion tab and joining in the effort of *vindicating* the Cause! Radio Free Dixie is already informing people of the good news about being a descendent of a Confederate Veteran. Our targeted internet ads are doing more of the same and reaching people who, up to now, we have not reached. All these ads are pointing folks to our web site where they can view videos, hear lectures, and read articles that give our side of the story—something most of these people have never heard before. These radio and internet ads can be downloaded by local SCV camps and run in their local media market. If every SCV camp would begin running these ads in addition to what is already being done by the Confederate Legion, we would cover the

South with positive information about our wonderful heritage and make the Sons of Confederate Veterans a commonly recognized organization and force to be dealt with.

Think of what will happen when feeble and submissive community leaders recognize that WE, the SCV, are now a powerful force for Southern Rights. Think of the positive results for our Cause when weak politicians recognize that they must deal faithfully with us or face a loud public outcry that will resonate at the ballot box! They may not love us but if they fear what we can do because of our influence, they will be hesitant to "stab us in the back" as they have done in the past.

The main message I want to pass on to my compatriots of the SCV is that, things are beginning to change, both in the United States and in the world. The tide is right, let us launch the ship of Confederate Vindication while the waters are right. Join and support the Confederate Legion!

The More Things Change

The following article was written in the mist of the Obama Administration when conservatives thought "it can't get worse!" With the election of Trump many believed that at last the tide was turning against Deep State big government advocates—they soon discovered just how deep "Those People" have entrenched themselves in Washington. The bogus election of 2020 should enlighten all Americans that standard politics is not the answer to the Yankee Empire's Federal tyranny. In the political arena, just like in the SCV's struggle defending Southern heritage, if we don't change our tactics and engage the enemy in a different manner, we will continue getting the same results. We cannot keep doing the same old thing over and over and expect to get a different result!

French journalist and literary critic, Jean-Baptiste Alphonse Karr, is noted for his epigram "The more things change, the more they stay the same." Karr would surely agree that in the 20th and 21st century, American politics reflects his little truism.

In November of 1968 Southern conservatives were ecstatic when Richard Nixon was elected president. We were assured that now things would get better since someone other than big government Democrats were in the White House. How did that turn out for America in general and the South in particular? It was Nixon that pushed forced busing upon the South, not to better educate Southern students but to appease the NAACP. The heinous result lives on to this date as education had to take a back seat to social engineering—remember that all schools in the South were open to anyone regardless of color before Nixon's forced busing. In the style of a Marxist tyrant, Nixon imposed price and wage controls on many aspects of America's so-call free market economy. Nixon continued LBJ's Great Society big government drive by imposing upon Americans such power grabbing bureaucratic agencies as the Environmental Protection Agency (EPA).

In November of 1980 once again we all celebrated the victory of a real conservative, Ronald Reagan. Without a doubt Reagan has proved to be the best president in my lifetime (Truman through Obama). He was elected on a platform of lower taxes, less government, States' Rights, and strong national defense. Yet when he left office, the Federal government had not been reduced but had grown in size and power. None of the big government policies that touched Southerners had been rolled back.

In November of 1994 conservatives again celebrated as Newt Gingrich and associates won control of the U.S. House of Representatives for the first time in four decades. Was big government rolled back? Were we the people at the local level given tools to defend our rights against a runaway big government? No!

After Gingrich's "conservative revolution" and several "conservative" Republican presidents, America is now straddled with Obama! "The more things change, the more they stay the same." Or in the case of Southerners, they just keep getting worse. The power of big government cannot be reduced as long as we keep doing the same thing over and over and expecting a different outcome. No matter who wins in the next November election, we will get the same results as we did with Nixon, Reagan, Bush, Gingrich and add whatever name you like to follow. Washington is the problem; quit looking to Washington to fix the problem—it's not a problem to them, it's how they get rich! As explained in Ron Kennedy's booklet, *Dixie Rising: Rules for Rebels,* there is a path to victory in both the Southern heritage struggle and the political redemption of our government.

Chapter IV

THE FIGHTING SPIRIT

The present-day continuation of cultural genocide is necessary to justify Yankee aggression and maintain the unholy alliance between Northern liberals...and Southern Scalawags.

NO AMERICAN MILITARY FORCE has ever displayed the long-term fighting spirit as was displayed by the men of the Confederate military. Until this present age of anti-South, cultural genocide, the U.S. military embraced the Southern soldiers' élan as both a model for its military and a unique quality of America's fighting men. Photographs of the Confederate flag being displayed by American troops can be found for every war the United States has fought since the end of the War for Southern Independence. But as we all know only too well, "things they are a-changing." Fifty-seven years ago, President John F. Kennedy, while standing near a Confederate Battle Flag, stated: "As a New Englander, I recognize the South is the land of Washington...Jefferson...and Robert E. Lee... ." Today there are very few politicians in the South, let alone in Washington, DC, that would repeat President Kennedy's words. The very idea of being photographed near a Confederate Flag is totally out of the question for the ruling elite in Washington.

According to the reports the Heritage Operations Committee is monitoring, there are from 2 to 10 negative news reports issued to the general public each day of the week. If you are wondering why even in the South there are Southerners who no longer respect Southern heritage, consider the fact that the average Southerner gets his information from anti-South media. Additionally, most Southern students are taught this same negative narrative in schools and colleges; furthermore, mainline religious groups are now jumping on the "hate the sinful South" bandwagon and one begins to understand the gravity of our situation. We of the "Baby Boomer" generation have lived long enough to see a loving pride in the South reduced to the public destruction of Confederate memorials. If something is not done to give a more positive view of Southern Heritage, all monuments and memorials to the Confederacy will be labeled as a Nazi-like symbol of hatred and racism. Presently, a majority of Americans (55%) and an even larger majority of Southerners (70%) view Southern heritage in a positive light but those numbers are decreasing each year. When a majority of the public agrees with the neo-Marxist, false narrative of the South, even Confederate displays on private property will be labeled a "public nuisance" and have to come down—majority rule, you know.

That's the bad news but thankfully there is some very good news also! A completely new SCV approach to these attacks is beginning to "take back the narrative" and turn the tide back to sanity and respect for Southern heritage and traditional American values. Commander Gramling's 'Southern Victory Campaign' is beginning to have a positive effect but this effort will not be successful without your help and the help of the local SCV camps. The Heritage Operations Committee has begun its job of establishing tools to be used by BOTH the national organization and the local camps. As I have stated in previous 'Forward the Colors' articles, we have built and put on line our new web site, Make Dixie Great Again, collecting and making pro-Confederate videos, running internet and radio ads (Radio Free Dixie and Internet Free Dixie), and making our existence known to the political establishment via such tactics as our Smithsonian Rebuttal effort.

These are just some of the things that we are doing at the SCV National level but these efforts alone are virtually useless without the support of our membership at the local level. As has been done in the month of February with our Confederate Diversity Month, the Heritage Operations Committee of the National SCV will push other pro-South messages during this year. At this time, Heritage Operations can only buy approximately 300 ads to promote this positive narrative of the South. Nevertheless, these ads are being made available to each SCV camp and Division. Just think of the positive response we could get if every SCV camp, imbued with the fighting spirit of their ancestors, would download these ads (available at the Make Dixie Great Again web site) and buy air time on their local radio station. Here are two big questions for each SCV member and each SCV camp: (1) "Do we want to give our enemies a real fight or do we simply want to talk about the fight?" (2) Are those who talk-the-talk willing to walk-the-walk? I have been a member of the SCV for over thirty years. During that time one fact has always been made clear: The major work of the SCV is done at the camp level. Yes, the National Headquarters must provide the tools and information necessary to carry on the work of the SCV but headquarters is a long way from your local camp.

The main question being asked of the Heritage Operations Committee by SCV members is, "What can I do to help take back the narrative?" I have been very impressed by the numbers and the passion of our members who have displayed this "Confederate" fighting spirit by asking this question. Do we have nay-sayers? Sure, there are always those who are first to find fault but last to take positive action—I dealt with this as president of my local Lion's Club and even in my church; the SCV is not different. Yet, even the nay-sayers can give us good insight into how better to promote our efforts and Vindicate the Cause for which our Confederate ancestors fought.

Here are some things you and your friends can do to advance this effort to turn the tide of anti-South propaganda: Join the Confederate Legion—otherwise we will not have funds necessary to take our pro-South message to the general public; identify local friendly or at least fair media outlets: radio, press, and T.V. stations. Here is what we need: Name of media and contact information, that is, e-mail, fax, phone, and physical address (town, zip code, state). This information will be used for placing positive ads in the media, releasing information from the SCV to the general public and arranging speaking engagements for members of the Heritage Operations Committee to address camp members about Commander Gramling's 'Southern Victory Campaign.' Please remember that EVERYONE on this committee is a volunteer; we do not have an expense account and we do not get paid for our travel expenses so please consider this when requesting a speaker. [*One year after the publication of this article, the SCV's GEC* *approved reimbursing the Chief of Heritage Operations for expenses he incurred directly related to promoting SCV heritage defense up to $3,000.00 per year.]*

Even if only a spark of that fighting spirit displayed by our ancestors is left within our soul, we can overcome the vicious, anti-South campaign of Cultural Genocide. I have seen that spark alive and well in the faces of thousands of our people as I have spoken to fellow Southerners. In more than just a few it is larger than a spark, it is more than a glowing ember, it is a white-hot flame. Even those Southerners who are not (yet) members of the SCV, UDC, OCR, or other pro-South groups, when given a positive view of their ancestors, they begin to glow with the fire of resistance to tyranny. We can win, WE MUST WIN. Join the Confederate Legion and let's Make Dixie Great Again!

DEATH BY EXPERTS

The following article was written in the mist of the Covid-19 pandemic. With the Federal and local governments trampling upon most if not all Constitutionally protected Rights without a unanimous and vigorous protest, one is left wondering if there is a "Fighting Spirit" left in America in general and the South in particular.

Walter D. Kennedy, BSN, RRT, CRNA

Watching events unfold as the non-pandemic/pandemic worked its way across the fruited plain has been an eye-opening experience. For those of us who have been warning Americans that the Constitution is nothing but a paper barricade against assaults of tyranny, we are vindicated—but this is not a source of joy. Many years ago, I had a good friend who loved cigarettes and regardless of what I told him, he insisted I was wrong. He quit smoking cigarettes a few months before he died but it was no fun telling him, "I told you so!" The same is true vis-à-vis the loss of Constitutional liberty that has become the "new normal" in the United States.

What happened to the "land of the free and home of the brave?" For many years true Constitutionalists sadly recognized that the Ninth and Tenth Amendments to the Constitution had become null and void. As we warned, all such limitations on tyrannical government will be destroyed when Big Government deems it necessary. But why have Americans so quickly "rolled over" and allowed our liberties to be trampled upon?

It seems that Americans have fallen victim to the disease of "Expertitis." To nullify all Constitutional restraints against tyranny, all the government has to do is parade before a frightened public one or more "experts," appropriately adorned in a white lab coat, who will inform the gullible that it is "necessary" for public safety to forget about the Constitution. Most modern (20th and 21st century) tyrants have employed "experts" proclaiming the necessity of the moment to advance their nefarious design of trampling upon liberty. Therefore, let us look into the advice given by "experts" and the role of "necessity" in promoting tyranny.

When considering the advice of experts, one must be aware of the fact that experts are not God and they are only dealing with the facts known or presumed by them at that time—they are not endowed with unlimited or unquestionable knowledge. Around the year 77 AD, Pliny the Elder gave this advice for treating a patient bitten by a rabid dog: "When a person has been bitten by a mad dog, he may be preserved from hydrophobia by applying the ashes of a dog's head to the wound...or insert in the wound ashes of hairs from the tail of the dog that inflicted the bite." Now you know where the term "Hair of the dog that bit you" came from. Pliny the Elder was one of Rome's most respected and admired scholars—the Dr. Fauci of the Roman Empire! He, like Fauci, was an expert—but experts can be wrong. When the Black Death was decimating Europe, many cures were advanced by experts. One of the most famous was the Bird-Beak mask. The mask was filled with flowers and other sweet-smelling objects in order to purify foul air which the experts said was the cause of the disease—but experts can be wrong. The mask supposedly offered protection from the deadly contagion—now where have I heard that before? During the 19th century, experts advised bleeding a sick patient to rid the patient of "bad blood." Until late in the 19th century, medical experts embraced the theories of the well-respected, Greco-Roman physician Galen, who followed the advice of Hippocrates, who practiced bleeding—but experts can be wrong.

Yes, we are talking about ancient times not modern-day experts. Surely, our modern-day, science-based experts cannot be blinded to reality. Yet, during my fifty-five years in the health-care profession, I have seen a lot of "expert" advice proven wrong. In 1965 it was not uncommon for recovery room patients to be administered carbon dioxide in order to stimulate respiration. The experts noticed that when one is exposed to a high volume of carbon dioxide, they respond by increasing ventilation. Well, it was soon discovered that a patient recovering from a general anesthetic is not a candidate for carbon dioxide—the experts were wrong! Long before the system of arterial blood gas analysis became common, the experts informed the world that the way to treat a COPD patient in respiratory crisis was to administer as much oxygen as possible and a few milligrams of morphine. The struggling patient would "pink-up" (improved oxygen content in blood) and become calm; too often, shortly thereafter, they would die. All of this was being done per the advice of the experts—but experts can be wrong. The preceding is but a very small sample of what I have witnessed in fifty-five years as a healthcare professional. The point is not that people were being willingly killed by experts but that even the most educated and up-to-date expert is not God!

With the advancement of science, new methods were discovered that added to the medical profession's incomplete knowledge about how to treat patients. With improved knowledge, corrections were made in treatment. But no change can be made if we suffer from an unquestioning addiction to the advice of "experts," because experts can be wrong. Remember, the experts said first that the corona virus is not a pandemic threat and then it was a pandemic threat. Experts said foreign travel should not be stopped, then they said it should. Experts said masks were not needed, now they say if you don't wear one you are a dangerous individual. Experts said that the best way to cut down on corona virus deaths was to lock-up everyone at home, now they tell us that this has caused an increase in corona cases. Experts told us that the corona virus lives for hours or days on any surface, now they tell us that is not true. Obviously, experts can be wrong!

Death due to corona virus is a sad reality for many individuals and families. Depending on whose statistics you use, the death rate from corona virus infection is less than one percent. If this is your family member or friend it is indeed sad but if we allow the "experts" to destroy the last few protections offered by the Constitution, that will be catastrophic for the current and future generations of Americans. Those who have desired the final destruction of the few liberties enjoyed by Americans have seized upon this crisis to finally gut what is left of the Constitution. As they are so wont to say, "Let no crisis go to waste."

Here is how the final destruction works. Get an expert to pronounce a coming epic holocaust that can only be solved by immediate governmental action. Although said action will trample upon the Constitution it is proclaimed "necessary" in order to protect the people from an impending disaster. To calm the nerves of those citizens who still believe in the Constitution, the government will remind them that these most necessary orders and edicts are "temporary." Beware of government when it tells you that it must employ "temporary" rules because they are "necessary." John Milton, in *Paradise Lost,* warns about the use of "necessity" as a means of advancing devilish deeds: "So spake the fiend, and with *necessity,* the tyrant's plea, excused his *devilish deeds"* [emphasis added].

Lincoln trampled upon the Constitution in the North because it was *necessary* to save the Union. Lincoln then waged a barbaric war upon men, women, and children of the South and impoverished the South for 150 years after his death, because it was *necessary* to make America one nation. Today when the "powers that be" shut down free expression, arrest priests, pastors, and anyone daring to attend church services, and when they prevent once free citizens from working, it is said that it must be done because it is *necessary.* Where is the First Amendment? The sad reality is that the First Amendment is no more self-enforcing than the Tenth Amendment. Without REAL States' Right there is no way to enforce any Rights of "we the people" against an all-powerful Federal Empire. But sadder still is the reality that most State governments are nothing but sycophants, toadies, or better yet, lap dogs, of the Federal Empire. As General Lee pointed out, with the defeat of the South, Real States' Rights were lost. As General Lee noted, America would become "aggressive abroad and despotic at home." While most Southerners understand that the new, post-Appomattox Federal government had become aggressive abroad, they nevertheless have not fully embraced Lee's prediction of a "despotic at home" United States government. A review of what has taken place as a result of the "necessary" measures taken by an all-powerful government should be a wake-up call to all Americans.

Since Appomattox, every Southern State is ruled by a bayonet constitution—remember, this is what the native people of Hawaii called the constitution forced upon them after their legitimate government was overthrown by Yankee businessmen (see, ch. III, *Yankee Empire: Aggressive Abroad and Despotic at Home,* Kennedy, Shotwell Publishing). After Appomattox, the only state governments and state constitutions the South was allowed to have were those which paid homage and unquestioned allegiance to the indivisible Federal government. The South's post-Appomattox state governments were not based upon the consent of the governed but upon coercion, i.e., bloody bayonets. Is it any wonder that during this Corona overreach by the Federal government, no state has stood up to the Federal government and said, "No, you have gone too far"? The sad reality is that "government by the consent of the governed" does not exist in the United States. If Wisconsin desires to be free of the Federal government and its association with the rest of the United States, can it leave the union? The answer is, no! The people's consent be damned. As Lincoln pointed out it is necessary to trample upon the people's right of government by the consent of the governed so the Union can be preserved! It should be obvious to everyone that "If you can't leave, you are not free."

Those of us who believe that liberty is more important for this and future generations than life itself have our work cut out for us. We often think that the problem is with the Federal government. As this pandemic demonstrates state governors, who are nothing less than toadies of the Imperial Federal power, are just as dangerous as their Big Brother handlers. To save liberty we must rethink how to go about forcing our state governments to kowtow to *us* rather than Big Brother in Washington. Once that has been accomplished, we must retake or replace the all-powerful, indivisible Federal government. As a starter, I would suggest reading, *Dixie Rising: Rules for Rebels*. It's late, but not too late to save that little freedom upon which we now barely subsist before it too shall be taken from us.

There are three points being stressed herein. First, experts are not God, they have limited information and must act and react to newer information. Therefore, it is not an evil plot to question an expert and make him prove his theories. Second, be wary and cautious of politicians who declare that an otherwise detrimental act must be tolerated because of "necessity." Third, be extremely leery of political leaders, who in combination with experts, use the necessity of the moment to cancel or otherwise nullify long-held Rights. The most fundamental rule in medicine is "First, do no harm." The same rule must be applied and enforced upon our elected officials if freedom is to survive.

Chapter V

CONFEDERATE COUNTER-ATTACK

WITH THE ONGOING ATTACK upon all things Confederate and the usual results of Dixie "getting the short end of the stick," it's time for some good news. First, congratulations to our compatriots in Arkansas for defending their State Flag with its Confederate memorial star. In Mississippi the minions of neo-Marxist political correctness have been stymied in their effort to remove the "Confederate" image from their State Flag. Not only that, one of the largest Mississippi State Flags in the State has been raised on the side of a major interstate highway in South Mississippi. In Texas, I recently took part in celebrating the opening of a memorial along a major interstate highway which consists of not only flags of the Confederacy but a beautiful monument. These are just a small sample of what is going on all across the Confederation. Hopefully we will soon have a better communication system within the SCV that will allow us to learn about these types of events before they take place. Through lack of information, we often deceive ourselves into thinking that "nothing is being done." A lot is being done but as we all understand, a heck-of-a-lot more *must* be done if we are to vindicate the Cause of the South.

Commander-in-Chief Gramling has instructed the Heritage Operations Committee to begin our SCV Counter-Attack upon the enemies of the South. As such we have executed two "Counter-Attacks." Our Counter-Attack is an effort by the SCV to put the general public and any detractor on notice that we will not "roll over and take it" when our heritage and rights are attacked. First and foremost, we want to get our positive message about the South before the people of America in general and the people of Dixie in particular. As such, in response to a slanderous article published by the *Smithsonian Magazine,* the SCV sent a letter to the *Smithsonian Magazine* demanding equal time for the Southern perspective. Not surprisingly, we got turned down but we also sent letters to members of Congress from Southern States as well as Governors of Southern states explaining our feelings about the Smithsonian's slander of the South. Many replies have been received from Congressional offices inquiring about who we (SCV) are and why we were upset. The result of these letters is to begin the process, and yes, we understand that it is just the beginning of the process, of making the Sons of Confederate Veterans a known and ultimately respected (maybe even feared) organization.

For the first time in SCV history, Commander Gramling proclaimed February as Confederate Diversity month. The Heritage Operations Committee has produced videos about Confederate diversity as seen in 'Commander's Comment' on our Make Dixie Great Again (MDGA) website. Other videos and articles are also on the website to educate and enlighten those who desire to know about the SCV and our stand on making Dixie great again. During the month of February over $6,000.00 in ads, radio and internet, have been and are still running across the South. These ads proclaim to the general public who we are and they give a positive message about the South. In addition, these ads point people to our new website, Make Dixie Great Again, where more information about Confederate diversity and the SCV can be found.

As we have always insisted, the Heritage Operations Committee cannot buy enough ads to tell John Q. Public our side of the story and thereby retake the narrative. But I am happy to announce that many local SCV camps have caught the fighting spirit and have downloaded our ads (available on MDGA website) and bought time on their local radio stations. One camp in North Louisiana even arranged for all the ads on MDGA website to be played as Public Service Announcements—that is, the ads are free! Some things can be done that do not cost money but have a very positive impact on getting our message out to the general public. We have asked camps to download a form letter to be sent to local churches and ministers. These letters inform the leaders of churches about the SCV's diversity campaign which includes religious diversity. Again, it must be pointed out that just because one does not get a positive response, it is still important to begin the process of making the name of the SCV known and respected. It will take longer for some to come around to respecting Southern heritage and some may never do so but we must make the effort. Also, each SCV member who uses social media and each SCV camp that uses social media needs to post information about the activities of the SCV. When we have new Commander's Comments, video, or a new "Counter Attack" effort, you can post that information on your social media. Share SCV information with friends who may or may not be SCV members. One thing that is simple and only costs a few dollars to do is buy extra copies of the *Confederate Veteran* magazine and drop one off at any waiting room you may visit, from your doctor's office to the local garage. People sitting around these waiting rooms will see and read something about the SCV that up until then they may have never heard.

As faithful members of the SCV sometimes we forget that a large number of fellow Southerners do not even know what the SCV is all about. This point was driven home to me recently while doing an extensive interview at Lee Circle in New Orleans. While setting up for an outdoor interview in front of what remained of the Lee Monument, the camera crew and host, all Northerners, were almost mobbed by a local construction crew wanting to know "what is going on?" When told that the camera crew was from Pennsylvania and doing a story on the removal of General Lee's monument, the construction crew began a vigorous and energetic denunciation of the act of removing the monument. This unsolicited defense of Confederate monuments was a shocking surprise to these Northerners. When the interviewer asked these workmen if they belonged to "Mr. Kennedy's organization," they not only said they did not but they did not know anything about the "Sons of Confederacy." As was pointed out in 'Forward the Colors' in the previous issue of *Confederate Veteran,* most Southerners support a positive display of Southern heritage. The problem is they are not organized and remain passive supporters and not active supporters. It is not the fault of these workers that they had little or no knowledge of the SCV, it is OUR FAULT! If we are to save our heritage from ultimate and final destruction, we must do those things necessary to get our message and our name (SCV) outside of our small group.

We must take our message to John Q. Public. This cannot be done without your support. Join the Confederate Legion and encourage others to do so. Without the funds generated by membership in the Confederate Legion, we cannot buy ads and continue to create and post videos. Encourage your camp to get involved in promoting these ads and other projects that will help get our message to John Q. Public. It would be a shame and disgrace to this generation of Sons of Confederate Veterans to allow the neo-Marxists to walk all over our heritage when we have the support of 65% to 70% of our fellow Southerners. All that is lacking is the will to get involved.

Getting everyone involved is on our agenda. In the coming weeks and months, you may be hearing from several members of the SCV's Heritage Operations Committee. These men will be assisting in implementing the various aspects of Commander Gramling's Southern Victory Campaign. Everything from our new website, videos, ads, and Confederate Counter-Attacks are part of Commander Gramling's vision to "take back the narrative." Most SCV members know the men holding the three top positions of this committee: Walter D. Kennedy, Carl Jones, and James R. Kennedy. The others may not be so well known but they have vital tasks to perform for the SCV. Brian McClure of Ruston, La., is in charge of Communication and Networking. Many armies and nations have gone down in defeat because of a lack of good communication. You will be hearing from Mr. McClure in the future about what your division and camp can do to help in putting the SCV into the 21st century communication network. Ray Shores, of Flora, Miss., is a man you don't see often because he is on the reverse side of our cameras. Mr. Shores is responsible for our videos, radio ads, targeted internet ads, and marketing efforts. Dr. Sandy Mitcham, of Monroe, La., well respected author (with over 40 books published on WWII and the War for Southern Independence) and professor of history (retired), will be giving the Heritage Committee guidance on the historical accuracy of anything we publish via any media. The Heritage Committee also has three men, one from each SCV Army, to assist in strategic planning and tactical support. The members of the Strategic Planning & Tactical Support team are as follows: Loy Mauch, Ark.; Tom Hiter, KY; Mike Scruggs, NC. Please work with these men when they contact you so we can all work together to

MAKE DIXIE GREAT AGAIN! DEO VINDICE

TOO MUCH TRUTH FOR THE *USA TODAY*

If more proof was needed that Southerners must go on the offensive if we are to save our Southland, the rejection of this short Op-Ed is more such proof. As the mobs of radical neo-Marxists were desecrating and destroying one Confederate monument after the other, a reporter for the USA Today Newspaper asked if I would write a short article more or less giving a view from the South of this madness. While the USA Today gleefully reported on the destruction of Confederate monuments, this article "never saw the light of day" from the leftist media. As so often noted, our story does not fit their narrative, thus, we must take back the narrative.

Watching the destruction of monuments to American heroes distresses all fair-minded individuals. We do not honor America's heroes because they were perfect, rather, we honor them because they were exceptional. Our heroes, Lee or Grant, Lincoln or Davis, deserves our respect. The Sons of Confederate Veterans are committed to honoring America's heroes. We also completely reject the false premise that Confederate monuments were erected as symbols of racism and/or treason. Confederate monuments honor a very diverse group of men and women and are symbols of inclusion not division.

As historian C. Vann Woodward noted, "Jim Crow was born in the North." The United States Supreme Court, not a Southern Court, made Jim Crow the law of the land in 1896. The Court's decision was based upon an 1854 *Massachusetts* law that segregated Black and White children. The only justice voting against Jim Crow was a Southerner. Rather than being intimidated by a Confederate monument, Mississippi's Black Representative, John Harris, and all African American representatives, spoke in favor of funding a Confederate monument in Jackson, Mississippi. On the floor of the Mississippi House of Representatives Harris stated, "I too wore the Gray!" Confederate monuments honor ALL Confederates! We also reject the false narrative of Confederates as traitors. America was founded upon an act of secession in 1776. Remember, British Unionists slandered American patriots, as "rebels and traitors."

After losing its independence, the people of the South were reduced from prosperity and health to poverty and disease. We were punished with poverty and now must endure neo-conservatives such as Levine and Hannity parroting the leftist narrative about the "Jim Crow South" and "Confederate treason." Fellow Americans take note, Southerners are the only minority in America who have their history and culture defined by their enemies. We are witnessing the Yankee Empire's "final solution" attempt of Southern cultural genocide. Southerners are beginning to ask, "Are Southerners being treated as equals with other Americans or as a defeated and occupied nation?"

Chapter VI

THE SCORPION'S STING

IN 1824, VIRGINIA'S GREAT ORATOR and statesman, John Randolph of Roanoke, proclaimed, "When the scorpion's sting is probing us to the quick, shall we stop to chop logic?" At that time in American history, Southerners were beginning to understand that the North was using its growing control of the Federal Government to enrich itself while impoverishing the South. Randolph was restating Patrick Henry's warning of the South becoming the "milch cow" of the Union. As both Henry and Randolph noted, endlessly discussing (chopping logic) the original intent of the Constitution could not offer any relief as the scorpion's sting of Northern domination was "probing us to the quick." When a scorpion is stinging, that is not the time to contemplate "what did I do to cause this," or "what is the environmental impact of my killing this creature." What is needed is action, quick and effective action.

Today, more than any time in the history of these United States of America, traditional American values are under attack. As we in the SCV warned our fellow citizens, the Confederacy is just the "low-hanging fruit" that neo-Marxists will go after first. Once they have established a tradition of taking down anything the neo-Marxists can associate with slavery, racism, the Confederacy, and the South, they will then move on to taking down all traditional American values. Here are a few cases to demonstrate this anti-American assault: Led by the president of San Francisco's Board of Education, an effort is in place to remove an eighty-three-year-old, 1,600 square-foot mural of George Washington. The same class of cultural bigots who demand the removal of all things Confederate are discovering "insults and offenses" by having to view a memorial to George Washington. The attacks of the Cultural Gestapo are even reaching such wholesome individuals as Kate Smith, known around the world for her performance of "God Bless America." Mrs. Smith has a long history of promoting and defending the civil rights of African American singers and performers. In the days of black-and-white TV, Kate Smith defied Hollywood and invited Josephine Baker (1951) and the Billy Williams Quartet (1952), Black entertainers, to appear on her weekly TV show. Nevertheless, the Cultural Gestapo is determined to destroy Smith because back in the 1930s, she recorded two songs that some people find offensive today. These are the same tactics that are used against the SCV and all things Confederate.

The Cultural Gestapo is indeed "probing us to the quick" and this is not the time to stop and "chop logic.' This is the time for ACTION.

I am happy to report that we are winning some very important battles against the Cultural Gestapo. For example, in Tennessee several legislative victories were reported to me, including preventing the watering down of SCV Tag funding for WBTS flag restoration; defeat of an attempt by anti-South elements to gerrymander committees in the legislature to favor their perverted view of Dixie; and the securing of proper representation in appropriate House and Senate committees to prevent stacking committees with anti-South elements. In Virginia, a judge ruled that statues of Confederate Generals Robert E. Lee and Stonewall Jackson are indeed war memorials and cannot be removed at will by the city of Charlottesville. During April, Confederate History Month, numerous towns, cities, and states, as well as many organizations, have recognized Confederate Heroes with celebrations, news releases, and showing of the Colors of the Confederacy. On a windy Thursday afternoon this past April, I joined over a dozen men of three different SCV camps on a bridge across the Ouachita River in North Central Louisiana as we "showed the Colors" to thousands of homeward bound fellow citizens. From one end of that long bridge to the other, one could hear horns blowing in approval, see smiles, and thumbs-up, also passengers and drivers waving their approval. Yes, we did have a few negative looks and hand gestures! But those could be numbered on one hand, whereas the positive responses were impossible to count.

Over and over in the past few months, the Heritage Operations Committee has been explaining that at this time we have the vast majority of people on our side. Even a majority of non-Southerners agree with us! A 2015 CNN Poll (not exactly a pro-South news outlet) found that 57% of Americans do NOT view the Confederate Flag as an evil symbol but as a symbol of Southern pride. In 2017, an NPR/PBS News Hour poll discovered that 62% of Americans (North and South) believed that Confederate Monuments should NOT be removed. A recent Tennessee poll found that 84% of respondents favored leaving Confederate Monuments alone while an LSU poll demonstrated similar results in Louisiana. The natural question to ask is, "With such positive support, why are our monuments and flags coming down?" Once again, let me explain why we are losing so many fights to keep our heritage alive and well. Community leaders who quickly turn their backs on our heritage are responding like Pavlov's dog. These scalawags are acting with a conditioned reflex, with no forethought. They are taught (conditioned) that Southerners offer little or no expense to their agreeing with our neo-Marxist enemies. If they thought a well-organized organization would put the spotlight of negative public opinion upon them, they would be less likely to surrender to the neo-Marxists. When the SCV can put fear into weak or spineless community leaders, then, and only then, will they find the courage to "do the right thing." With rare exceptions, politicians will follow the path of least resistance. Until now defenders of Dixie were not displaying much of a threat to community leaders. But those days are coming to an end--it's time to Make Dixie Great Again!

So how will we put fear of us into our political and community leaders? Remember the polls I cited. These polls are only a few of many such polls which prove we have the public on our side. We must EDUCATE to MOTIVATE to ACTIVATE our fellow Southerners. That 57% of Americans and that 65% to 75% of Southerners who agree with us are passive in their support. Yes, they will wave and give us a thumbs-up when they see us showing the Colors but will they write letters to their representatives or call their community leaders and complain about the threatened removal of a Confederate Memorial? Will they vote against those who support the removal of Confederate Memorials? No, for the most part the thumbs-up, smiling, waving supporters are passive in regard to positive action. Using our educational efforts, we must motivate these Southerners and put them in a frame of mind to become activists in defense of our Heritage and Rights. How then shall we make active supporters out of passive supporters?

One thing is for sure, if we continue doing what we have been doing for the past forty years, we will continue suffering one defeat after another. This is why Commander Gramling has instituted the "Southern Victory Campaign." The SCV must go on the offensive and give our fellow Southerners the good news about our Southland or they will become deluded sheep following the neo-Marxist mantra. Commander Gramling's Southern Victory Plan is designed to educate to motivate to activate Southerners. Therefore, he established the Confederate Legion (CL) which is now running radio and internet advertisements promoting a positive view of the South. These ads point people to our new website, Make Dixie Great Again: www.makedixiegreatagain.com. On this website more positive information about the South in the form of videos, articles, and radio ads can be viewed and responded to. This past month the Confederate Legion has bought over $5,500.00 in radio ads and $1,000.00 in internet ads promoting the SCV and a positive view of the Confederacy. Ron Kennedy, Deputy Chief of Heritage Promotions, speaking for the SCV's new effort was interviewed on the Michael Berry Show. Michael Berry's Show is syndicated across the South and nationally on the internet. But the SCV needs you and your camp to help.

IT'S TIME FOR A COUNTER-ATTACK

Every two months the CL is sponsoring a new "**Counter-Attack.**" Starting in February our first **Counter-Attack** was about Confederate Diversity. In April and May the **Counter-Attack** focused on Confederate Veterans as American Veterans. In June-July the **Counter-Attack** will focus on July 4^{t,h} America's Secession Holiday. Similar **Counter-Attacks** will continue throughout the year with appropriate ads and videos pushing a positive narrative about our Southland. But this cannot be done without your assistance. If you are tired of always being attacked and never striking back, now is the time for action. With every **Counter-Attack,** each SCV camp can go to MDGA website and download one or more of our one-minute radio ads and take them to your local radio station and buy air time for these ads. An action element is included with each **Counter-Attack.** An action element is usually a sample letter from your local SCV camp to various members of the local community. The action element for the April-May **Counter-Attack** consisted of a letter to be sent to the local American Legion, VFW, and other local community leaders. Every SCV camp should become a member of the CL and encourage its members to join also. It is the membership fees from joining the CL as well as generous donations that provide the funds to keep our **Counter-Attacks** going. Ninety percent of each dollar collected is used to buy radio and internet ads, promoting a positive view of the South. Membership is open to anyone who is willing to donate to the Cause of the South. We already have many non-Southerners who are happy to help in defending the Cause of the South.

Yes, my fellow Southerners, the scorpion's sting is probing us to the quick! We can stand around and chop logic, that is, endlessly debating why The South Was Right and how this or that Confederate unit or leader was superior to others, or we can get busy and take action against those who are "probing us to the quick." Go to our website, view the videos, and listen to the radio ads, and start the process in your community of educating to motivate to ACIVATE!

As noted in the previous article, when the scorpion's sting is probing one to the quick, it's time to do more than just talk. The following article also points out how the South is routinely mistreated by the victorious North and challenges Southerners to become more than America's "low-peck hen."

DIXIE AND THE LOW-PECK HEN

For those of us who were raised on a farm or who currently own chickens, understanding the plight of the "low-peck hen" is almost common knowledge. For those unfamiliar with the social order of chickens, let me explain. Within every flock of chickens there is a "pecking" order. The pecking order starts with the highest chicken that can peck everyone below her but no one pecks her. The order descends, by order of the next chicken, to the lowest hen that everyone can peck on but since she is the lowest hen, she has no one to peck on, thus, the term, "low-peck hen."

While watching my chickens I noticed how my low peck-hen, while minding her own business and not bothering anyone, was brutally attacked by one of her "superiors." As I watched this little act of chicken society work itself out, I could not help but feel sorry for the chicken being attacked but I was also painfully reminded that, as a member of a defeated and occupied nation (The Confederate States of America), I too was a low peck hen! Consider the South back in the summer of 2015, minding its own business and not harming anyone, when a deranged youth in Charleston, S.C., committed what everyone considered a horrible act. Like my little low peck hen, the South and all things Confederate were instantly, brutally attacked. The distasteful reality is that the defeated and the occupied South exists so as to provide America with its low-peck hen. Many times, I have heard fellow Confederates question the rationale of Yankees forcing Southerners to remain in the Federal government "if they hate us so much." As every empire understands, it can be very politically useful to have a defeated and occupied people to kick around from time to time.

Unfortunately, most Southerners today are blind to the misuse and mistreatment of Southerners by the victorious Yankee. For the past 150 years the South has been America's low-peck hen. Modern Southerners cannot imagine any other existence for the South than that of America's low-peck hen! After all, "it's always been like this." No, my fellow Southerners, it has not always been like "this." Only after Appomattox and the defeat of the real American republic of republics by the Federal Empire has it been like "this." My poor, mistreated low-peck hen has it better than we Southerners, at least her children will not inherit her status but the children of the South will always be the Yankee Empire's low-peck hen. Do you want your children and grandchildren to become the Yankee Empire's "low-peck" hen? This generation of Southerners can become the wave of the future and give Real American Liberty a nation to live in with a people who love it.

Chapter VII

BETSY ROSS, THE RACIST?

FOR MANY YEARS the Sons of Confederate Veterans has been proclaiming to our fellow Americans that the neo-Marxist attack upon all things Confederate will not stop at the eradication of Confederate history. The recent (July 2019) attack upon the so-called "Betsy Ross" United States Flag is just the most recent assault against Traditional American Values. Within the past two months a mural of President George Washington has been scheduled for removal; the celebration of Thomas Jefferson's life in his home state was canceled; other United States presidents such as both Roosevelts and William McKinley have been deemed as unworthy of respect; John Wayne and Kate Smith have been banished; and to top it all off, in Oregon a statue honoring Oregon's Pioneers is being taken down. The preceding does not even touch upon the numerous depraved assaults against Christian symbols. Yes, the SCV was RIGHT! The attack against our heritage is just the tip of the iceberg of the neo-Marxist assault against Traditional American Values.

The sad fact is that the assault against our heritage is having a very negative effect upon our ability to defend our Rights and heritage. Today, the neo-Marxist narrative of a hate-filled, racist, slave-defending South is accepted and embraced by more and more Americans—including Southerners. Thirty years ago, Southerners, by an overwhelming majority (90% to 95%) had a positive opinion of Southern heritage and history. Today that number has dropped to between 65% to 70% and the downward movement is accelerating in an ever-increasing pace. If current trends continue, in ten years we may be facing a Southern population where the majority of citizens hold a negative view of the traditional South. The implication of this is shocking. Think what will happen once a majority of the citizens of the South view our heritage in a negative way. At that time political pressure will be applied to banish all things Confederate claiming such symbols are hate speech—don't think that your First Amendment "free speech" Rights will be protected. Our enemies will no more respect the First Amendment than they currently respect the Tenth Amendment.

We are often told that if Confederate monuments cannot be maintained on public property, we should move them to private property. That will not last for long! When the neo-Marxists' view of the South is the *new* norm, they will simply declare Confederate flags and monuments to be an unsightly "public nuisance" and have them removed from public view. If the Federal government can regulate unsightly automobile junkyards (23 U.S. Code) or regulate where and what type of billboard can be placed on U. S. highways (Highway Beautification Act, 1965), don't think that Confederate monuments and flags will be safe from the wrath of raging neo-Marxist radicals. One thing I discovered when interviewing friends in the billboard business, is that they maintain that "regulate" is too mild a word to use as it relates to their business and the Feds.

The main threat to our existence as a unique culture, that is, Southern culture, is the continuing decrease in the number of people who are willing to speak up and defend the Cause of the South. Many people run away from defending the Cause of the South because they have bought into the narrative that defenders of the South are hate-mongers. Other people would like to defend their family's history but are unsure of the facts of history. Still other people understand the truth of our history but are afraid that "I am the only one who feels this way!" This latter cause for inaction is the most common expression that Ron and I have heard from people who have read *The South Was Right!* Here is how the Kennedy Twins have heard people state the issue: "I am more than willing to "help" in this fight but I just cannot 'fight by myself.'" The good news is, "They are not alone." The bad news is that so many do not understand that we, the SCV, are able and willing to work with them in defense of our heritage and families.

This point was driven home to me back in January 2019. At that time, I was asked to go to New Orleans to assist in an interview on the removal of General Lee's statue at Lee Circle in New Orleans. A Yankee T.V. crew of about five people plus Ron and myself were walking close to where General Lee's monument once stood, and as you would expect, drawing a lot of attention by those in the area. Seeing the commotion, a nearby construction crew of about six men came over and asked the T.V. crew "What is going on?" When this Yankee reporter responded that they were making a film about the removal of Lee's monument, without hesitation, these men proceeded to lecture the Yankees on the wonderful qualities of General Lee and that "he should be replaced." The reporter was shocked and asked if these men were members of the Sons of Confederate Veterans. They were not and only one had any knowledge of the SCV. This, gentleman, is why we are losing this fight. We must go on the offensive, take back the narrative and let our people, especially the political leadership, know who we are and that we are not only capable but willing to fight for our Cause.

To take back the narrative simply means to make our view of Southern history and heritage the common view for Southerners. It simply means stemming the negative downward trend of the South and gaining new supporters by turning passive supporters into active supporters. Always remember, we have the home court advantage! Every empire that has conquered a nation understands that to maintain the empire's hold on a defeated people, the empire's narrative (point of view and rationale for invasion and control of the occupied nation) must be continuously advanced. The empire's pushing of its rationale for the empire's action creates within the subjugated population a humbled, crestfallen population that is very reluctant to oppose their oppressor. But on the other hand, with only a very little encouragement via pride in people and culture, the conquered people will resist the empire's domination. The potential advantage resides with the South, not with the neo-Marxist rabble.

What we see in the South today is an ongoing effort to keep Southerners on the "stools of everlasting repentance," thereby making them less likely to challenge their rulers. In the United States as a whole, neo-Marxists are also attacking Traditional American Values with the hope to do to the rest of the United States what Lincoln's cronies have done to the South. Finally, we don't have to sit back and take it any longer. You and your SCV Camp can now take part in our Confederate Counter Attack and with the assistance of other good Americans go on the offensive and defeat the neo-Marxists. If you and your camp are not members of the Confederate Legion, please join. Go to our website www.makedixiegreatagain.com and view our videos and share them on your social media. Get your camp involved by downloading our radio ads and have them played on your local radio stations. Every two months the Confederate Legion will sponsor a new Counter Attack, at which time we will have suggested letters for your camp to reproduce and send to local members of your community. All of this effort will increase the SCV "footprint" in your community. As knowledge of the SCV and its ability to Counter Attack our enemy increases, we will begin the process of "taking back the narrative." This can be done and it must be done NOW if we are to continue as a truly Southern culture. Victory is possible but it is not possible without your efforts.

The Death of Free Speech

The battle for the truth about American history and Southern history has many different facets. When Betsy Ross and her beautiful United States Flag come under attack, we must understand that all Traditional American Values are hated by neo-Marxists. As pointed out in the following article, the neo-Marxist rabble will use any methods to stop liberty-loving Americans from proclaiming the truth about America and especially the South.

What does two Islamic terrorists attempting to kill Texans who were drawing cartoons of Mohammed and the politically correct attacks upon Southern Rights have in common? Simply this, both are un-American, un-Constitutional, and an attack upon basic rights secured to us by our colonial forefathers.

In Texas the attack was violent, ending in the death of two would-be jihadists. More to the point, the target of the attack was not just an individual cartoonist but a system of freedom where everyone is allowed to express their religious and political values. As William Rawle noted in his 1825 textbook on the Constitution, "The foundation of a free government begins to be undermined when freedom of speech on political subjects is restrained; it is destroyed when freedom of speech is wholly destroyed." Rawle goes on to explain that the First Amendment protection of free speech is solely for the protection of "religious and political" speech. Unfortunately, the same folks who demand the right to condemn and control the publication of cartoons of Mohammed, are the same folks who are demanding the removal of all things Southern which might "offend" some people.

The agents of political correctness, like their Islamic-terrorist counterpart, believe they alone have the right to sit in judgment on the speech and actions of all unbelievers, i.e., those who do not hold to the politically correct view of the world. The actions of the politically correct terrorists can be just as violent and deadly as that of the Islamic terrorists.

When people express doubts about this statement, I challenge them to read, *Death by Journalism?* This book details the effort of a good Christian man who only sought to enlighten young people about the truth of the War for Southern Independence. Jack Perdue, a regional historian of the Greensboro, North Carolina, area, was asked to teach a "Southern History" course at Randolph Community College. The only problem was Jack's dedication to the truth ran counter to the politically correct mantra of a hate-filled South fighting only to enslave Blacks and destroy equality in America. A very politically correct reporter took it upon himself to destroy Jack's effort and within a year Jack Perdue died of a heart attack. The amazing thing is that the reporter never presented any facts about Jack or the class he was teaching. What was said was only half-truths twisted to make it sound like something never suggested by Mr. Perdue. When half-truths and twisting of half-truths was not enough, lies were enlisted to destroy Perdue's class and Mr. Perdue.

Death by Journalism? is a story that should be read for many reasons: (1) It informs us of the true nature and character of our enemies; (2) it points out that "those people" don't hate us because they don't understand us. "Those people" hate us because we dare to speak the truth. Truth is a very uncomfortable and inconvenient reality for "those people" who love to hate the South. Anyone who proclaims to the world that they believe in the right of government by the consent of the governed must be silenced; (3) and *Death by Journalism?* honors Jack Perdue, a brave and honorable warrior who fought the good fight, just as surely as did his Confederate forefathers.

Chapter VIII

YOUR YANKEE SHOT and YOUR FREEDOM

THE TERM "YANKEE SHOT" was often heard in the post-war South but has faded into obscurity in our so-called modern age—more's the pity. But at one time in the South a child's navel or bellybutton was referred to as a "Yankee Shot." Upon discovering their navel, children would ask their mom, "Momma, what is this thang?" (Yankee children would no doubt say "thing") and Mom would reply, "Why that's where the Yankees shot you, child."

Of course, everyone would laugh and enjoy a moment of hilarity with the young child but always remember that, "many a truth hath been said in jest." The reality is that every successive generation in the South has suffered from being "shot" by the Yankees. Today young Southern children will be born in a society where they have a 30-40% LESS life-time earning prospect than if they were born NORTH of the Mason-Dixon Line. Those young Southerners' society, where going to church is a common event and Christian charity is commonplace, will be ruled by a secular humanist society were "church-going" is an oddity and charity is replaced by a miserly, money-worshiping society. In Dixie Southerners will have a vote in the Federal Empire's Congress, but that vote will amount to very little when it comes to protecting their world-view, heritage, and freedom because the Christian worldview will always be out-voted in the Empire's Congress.

Not only did the shot fired by "those people," AKA Yankees, harm the life of every subsequent generation of Southern children but it went right through the Declaration of Independence and the United States Constitution. America's founding fathers gave us a unique formula for establishing a free government. They believed that the only LEGITMATE government was one based upon the free and unfettered CONSENT of the governed. Remove the free consent of a people from that formula and you are no longer a free American, you are a subject of an empire. Remember this the next time you see a child's "Yankee Shot."

With that thought in mind, let us remember that September is the month set aside by this nation to celebrate the United States Constitution. The most recent Confederate Counter-Attack by the Confederate Legion is designed to promote a proper understanding of our Constitution. Please take the time to look AND share our "Constitution" videos and articles that have been placed on our Make Dixie Great Again website, www.makedixiegreatagain.com. One of our videos will look at the Confederate Constitution and answer many questions about that document. For those wishing a more complete study of the Confederate Constitution, I suggest reading Dr. Marshall DeRosa's book titled, *The Confederate Constitution of 1861,* University of Missouri Press. In the introduction of this book, DeRosa explains; "The Southerners did not abandon constitutional government; to the contrary, they reaffirmed their commitment to constitutional government under the auspices of the Confederate Constitution." Let us all reaffirm our commitment to this form of government—a form our Colonial and Confederate Forefathers believed in and fought to secure. As has been noted, the old saying about a child's "Yankee shot" is seldom heard or understood in today's society. Sadly, the same thing can be said about a proper understanding of the United States Constitution and the Cause of the South.

Recently a video has been making the rounds on YouTube in which Confederate, Soviet Union, North Korea, and Cuban flags are displayed on a poster. When college-aged people were asked to point out the most "offensive" flag on the poster, it was the Confederate Flag that was picked. Our noble heritage is viewed by these people as more offensive than that of any communist country! To add insult to injury, many of these college-age people were Southerners! When asked why the Confederate Flag was more offensive than a communist flag, one respondent stated, "This is what we were taught in school." As goes the term "Yankee Shot," so goes our Southern Heritage, Rights, and Liberty. If we do not take advantage of the opportunity to take our positive, pro-South message to "John Q. Public," the Cause of the South will be viewed as more reprehensible than that of the

Soviet Union, Red China, North Korea, or any other such heinous government. We don't have a lot of time to get this message out, it must be done now or all things Southern will become a by-word for the most reprehensible form of government and society known to man. Gentlemen of the SCV, the time for words has passed, the hour for action has struck!

Here is how you and your SCV camp can strike back at our neo-Marxist enemy. Six times a year, every other month, the Confederate Legion sponsors a **Confederate Counter-Attack.** In July 2019, we produced videos, radio ads, and articles to support our Confederate Counter-Attack, "July 4th America's Secession Holiday." Three sixty-second radio ads were made and the Confederate Legion bought air time on many radio stations promoting this theme. We also posted these ads on our website and asked camps to download these ads and buy time on their local radio stations; we posted letters that SCV camps could download and send to local social groups and political leaders; and we created pamphlets and newspaper inserts which camps can use to get our message out to their local community.

Every two months the Confederate Legion sends out e-mail alerts to SCV camps asking each camp to get involved in these Counter-Attack efforts. If every camp in the SCV would do so, within the next two or three years, the name of the SCV would become a recognized force, respected by and loved by the 70% of Southerners who already agree with us, and, most importantly, feared by the weak-kneed, waffling, political establishment. We can make a difference but only if we become activists in the Cause of the South. Please join and support the Confederate Legion; insist that your camp become an activist camp and support each Confederate Counter-Attack; and tell other people about this effort.

I have had the pleasure of traveling across the South and even out West promoting this effort to, as Commander-in-Chief Gramling states, "Take Back the Narrative." Yes, if we don't take back the narrative, the only narrative Southerners will hear and embrace is the vicious, neo-Marxist falsehood of an evil Southland. As the YouTube video demonstrated, the process is well under way. In November 2019 the Confederate Legion will roll out another Confederate Counter-Attack titled, "The Real Thanksgiving." Starting in February

2020 and every two months thereafter, we will be pushing another Confederate Counter-Attack. This effort will help in shaping a better view and understanding of the Cause of the South and the SCV. But this effort is a two-part effort. One part is being done by the Confederate Legion which will provide the tools for each camp to use to increase knowledge of the Cause of the South and the SCV within their community. The second part depends upon the local SCV camp using those tools and taking the Counter-Attack to the enemy in their local community. Without the support of each SCV camp, we will not be able to "Take back the narrative." Remember, we Southerners have the home-field advantage when it comes to "Taking back the narrative." When you light your candle of truth in your community, it will disperse a lot of darkness. A little goes a long way when you have this advantage. It's time to light your candles of truth and set the fortress of arrogance and ignorance ablaze.

Republican: Lincoln or Jefferson

The following article is from a speech given at the SCV's Stephen D. Lee Institute in 2011. Like the previous article, this speech was designed to point out that Southerners have been in the forefront of establishing and defending America's system of liberty and freedom. With the 1865 success of the Lincoln revolution, the government of the United States was radically and illegally changed into a fundamentally different system of government. Although the name, institutions, and flag remained the same, the republic of America's Founding Fathers was no more. Nothing demonstrates this fact more than the contrast between a Jeffersonian republican and a Lincoln republican.

There is an old story told about an aged Confederate veteran who upon seeing his grandchildren growing up without a proper respect for his service took his grandson to the battlefield at Vicksburg, Mississippi. It was here that he and his compatriots had fought the Yankees to a standstill and since the government had just opened the site, he thought it would be well to give his grandson a tour of the old battlefield. Toward the end of the journey, they ended up near the Federal cemetery where many Yankees "lie still in Southern dirt." Until then his grandson had not been too impressed with the tour but seeing so many white crosses he exclaimed (many times) "grandpa look at all those dead Yankees!" After hearing this several times, grandpa looked into the eyes of his grandson and said "Yep there are a lot of dead Yankees out there but it ain't near enough of them out there!"

This year marks the twentieth year-anniversary of the publication of *The South Was Right!*. In 1991 when the first edition was published many, if not most, of our friends said that we would soon be in Federal prison for advocating sedition. Well, after over 125,000 copies—the Feds have not got us yet! Ron and I were new in the SCV (the SCV had between 10 to 15 thousand members at that time), and most of the so-called leaders of the SCV warned us about "saying those things." I was told that an effort was mounted to "purge" the SCV of un-American members such as the Kennedy Twins. They said anyone who called the War Between the States the "War for Southern Independence" was much too radical and would surely cause the organization to lose its tax-exempt status. The idea that the SCV would be associated with a lecture series about real States' Right such as "The Road to Secession" held this past December in Gilmer, Texas, or this conference held by the Stephen D. Lee Institute, would have shocked the socks (if not worse) off of many of the so-called leaders at that time. Yes folk, we have come a long way but now is not the time to stop and congratulate ourselves. More, much more must be done if we are to defend and promote our heritage—*liberty being our greatest heritage as Southerners and as Americans.* As Ron and I have always pointed out and as we have heard this weekend already, The South Was Right in 1861 because America was Right in 1776—Thanks be unto God!

It's time to consider this question: "What type of republican are you?" I am talking here about little "r" republican as in republican institutions, not as in George Bush Republican. Tonight, I will be discussing many political parties, some gone with the wind, some still here and some that need to be gone with the wind!

Federalist, Democratic-Republican, Whig, Republican, Democrat and numerous other so-called "third parties" populate our past and present. Yet these parties can usually be classified in two divergent groups: (1) Federal supremacists—who believe that only the Federal government has the right to judge whether or not it is acting according to the Constitution and (2) State supremacists—who believe that "we the people" of the sovereign states are the final arbiters as to the constitutionality of the acts of our agent the Federal government. As has been pointed out *ad infinitum,* and to the total distress of our opponents, these United States were recognized by Great Britain as free and independent STATES and each one was separately named as an independent state. Yet from the beginning of this nation there was a small but very loud and influential group of Americans who desired a large and strong, i.e., sovereign, central government. The first political party in America, The Federalists Party, was composed of just such men.

A Federal supremacist is one who believes that the Federal government or at least the American people in the aggregate, are, as a whole, sovereign. John Marshall was typical of those who believed that the Federal government was sovereign and Joseph Story typical of those who believed Americans in the aggregate formed a sovereign entity. Note that both men believed that sovereignty resided in the Federal government, that is, they believed in Federal supremacy. Early in American history these men were known as High Federalists. By contrast, the advocates of state supremacy hold that "we the people" of each individual state are sovereign. Therefore, original sovereignty resides with the people at the local or state level, not with the Federal government. The people of the sovereign state authorized the writing of their state's constitution. State supremacists believe that all law that touches the people must come from the people. The government of the state, acting as the agent of the sovereign community, called the people into convention to ratify or reject the Federal Constitution. The power of the Federal government, according to the Constitution, comes from a delegation of power that originally belonged to "we the people" of the sovereign states. The Federal government is a government of secondary, not primary sovereignty, and therefore it cannot be supreme. The Federal government is only supreme in those specific areas in which "we the people" of the sovereign states delegate said authority to it. Those delegated Federal powers must be exercised *"pursuant"* to the Constitution (Art. IV, supremacy clause). As noted in the ninth and tenth Amendments in all other areas "we the people" of the sovereign states hold supreme authority. Early in the history of America, people who held these views were known as weak (mild or moderate) Federalists or Anti-Federalists. Anti-Federalists were not opposed to the Federal government but they were opposed to a government of Federal supremacy.

Now let us take a look at the advocates of Federal supremacy. As has been noted, the first political group of Federal supremacists were members of the Federalists Party. Chief among these early high Federalists were men such as Alexander Hamilton of New York, John Adams of Massachusetts, and John Marshall of Virginia. As time and events progressed, the names of men such as Henry Clay of Kentucky, Joseph Story of Massachusetts, and Daniel Webster of Massachusetts were added. The generation following these men produced the most notable, or if you prefer the most notorious advocate of Federal supremacy, Abraham Lincoln. In addition to these individual advocates of Federal supremacy we must also add the name of two new political parties that also advocated Federal supremacy, the Whig Party and the Republican Party.

Both Whigs and Republicans believed in an energetic, strong, all-powerful and *indivisible* Federal government. Jean Bodin, a French political theorist in 16th century France, noted that sovereignty was indivisible and resided in the state. Supreme Federalists followed this philosophy but placed sovereignty in the Federal government. Whigs and Republicans generally followed Henry Clay's political philosophy known as the American System. Under the American System the Constitution was interpreted in such a manner as to allow the Federal government a free hand to do as it pleased to promote various industries and projects—known as "internal" improvement by Federal supremacists or "infernal" improvements by advocates of real States' Rights. These two views of how the Constitution should be interpreted were bound to lead to conflict.

Among the early conflicts between these two groups was the effort to establish a national banking system in the United States (1791). *The Federalists* said that the "promotion of the general welfare" and the "necessary and proper" clauses in the Constitution allowed congress to establish a national banking system. By reading the Constitution "loosely" the advocates of Federal supremacy could "read into" the Constitution "implied" powers and authority that were never actually delegated to the Federal government.

At or about the same time as the national bank controversy arose, another point of contention between these two groups began to play itself out. In 1798 the Alien and Sedition Act was passed by the Federalists in congress and President John Adams, a Federalist, signed it. This Act caused another conflict between the advocates of Federal supremacy and the advocates of state supremacy. Remember that the state supremacy advocates were Anti-Federalists States' Rights men who by this time were known as republicans. Under the Alien and Sedition Act anyone who spoke against the President or the Federal government could be hauled before a Federal judge and sent to prison for sedition. Political leaders, newspaper editors and any common citizen could be tried for sedition if he spoke against the President. Under this act a member of Congress was actually arrested and tried before a Federal Supreme Justice and convicted of sedition. The threat of an abusive Federal government was established early in our history and would soon grow into a government which General Lee described as one being "aggressive abroad and despotic at home."

More conflicts would come in the form of protective tariffs, Federal protection for American shipping, and Federal bounties for failing industries (long before AIG, Goldman Sacks, or GM). All these issues would see advocates of big government, that is, Federal supremacists, reading the Constitution in such a way as to authorize any and all legislation that would advance the well-being of their "special interest" clientele and patrons—not unlike the system of government we see in Washington today. Always remember that big government, big taxes, and big money always lead to big corruption—which is a formula for fascism. In 1960 President Dwight Eisenhower warned Americans about the danger of the Military Industrial Complex. Near that time, Albert Spear, Hitler's minister of industrial out-put, warned of a similar danger in his book *Inside the Third Reich*. Both the leader of the Allies in WWII and a leader of Nazi Germany warning the world about a close relationship between big government and big business. We should heed their warnings!

Now let's look at the advocates of REAL States' Rights or the state supremacists. As we noted these men for the most part came from the large body of Americans known as Anti-Federalists. At the most fundamental level, these men did not trust government, big or small. Typical of these men was John Taylor of Caroline. Taylor was so distrustful of government that he had little faith in even a written constitution or any system to check the abuse of power of government because as he stated, "Great power should never be granted in the first place." These men felt that the larger the government and the further removed from the citizen the seat of government was the less it could be trusted. Today big government is like a bull in a china closet. There are three views of this "bull in a china closet" analogy of big government. One view holds that the bull in the china closet is a good thing and if everyone would just be quiet and don't upset the bull, everything will be okay—you radical Southerners and Tea Party folks just need to shut-up and don't upset the bull. A second group looks at the bull in the China closet and tells us that the problem is that the bull is too big and needs to be put on a diet. The third group looks at the bull and says, "the bull does not belong in our china closet, it belongs in the barnyard keeping the cows happy." Anti-Federalists believe that by putting a ring in the bull's nose, that is, nullification, we can remove the bull from the closet and put him where he belongs. Now if the bull is so dumb as to break back into our china closet, we will use our ultimate weapon, secession, and kill the bull, have one heck of a barbeque and get another bull that will do as we say and not as it desires. This was possible as long as Anti-Federalists could use the tools of REAL States' Rights

Chief among the Anti-Federalists was a Virginian, Patrick Henry. Henry succinctly summarized the Anti-Federalist view of government when he stated, "The first thing I have at heart is American *liberty*, the second is American *union*." Americans, Anti-Federalists, and mild Federalists agreed with Henry's view of liberty and government. In a free society such as established by the Founding Fathers, liberty always trumps government. James Madison in Federalists Paper No. 43 noted, "The safety and happiness of society are the objects at which ALL political institutions must be sacrificed." James Kent of New York, not a founding father but an early American jurist and author of *Commentaries on American Laws,* published in 1826, noted how our Union (government) was to be maintained when he stated "...for on the concurrence and good will of the parts, the stability of the whole depends." Let's see now—"liberty first then union," "political institutions must be sacrificed in order to protect the safety and happiness of society," "concurrence and goodwill (NOT bloody bayonets) promotes stability of the whole." Looks like Mr. Lincoln did not get those memos!

Patrick Henry and John Taylor were known as the Old Republicans. Yet it was Thomas Jefferson, not Henry or Taylor, who arose as the standard-barrier for the republican cause. No doubt, that after the publication of the Kentucky and Virginia Resolutions of 1798, which was a States' Rights rebuff of the Alien and Sedition Acts and the Federalist Party in general, Jefferson's name became inextricably attached to the cause of limited government. Not only was Jefferson the author or at least chief editor of the Declaration of Independence but he also wrote the Kentucky Resolutions, which the State of Kentucky passed in 1798. In this document Jefferson clearly announces that it was the States that created the Federal government. Also, Jefferson tells us that the Federal government was not created to be the Lord and Master of the States but was to act as an agent of the States. Jefferson also points out that it is the right and duty of the State to judge for itself as to whether the Federal government is acting according to its charter, the Constitution. And finally, Jefferson in the Kentucky Resolutions and Madison in the Virginia Resolutions, declare that it is the duty of the State to act independently of the Federal government to protect the rights of its citizens—interposition, nullification, or whatever action the state deems necessary to provide for its citizens "safety and happiness" is a duty of the state.

With the emergence of the Republican Party in the late 1840s, the term republican began to take on the quality of a cuss word in the South and other parts of Democratic America. After the demise of the Federalist Party and the rise of the Democratic-Republican Party of Jefferson and Jackson, the advocates of big government, that is, the Federal supremacists, reemerged as Whigs. Chief among these Whigs was Henry Clay of Kentucky. Clay promoted his so-called American System which paralleled the economic/political policy of the Federalist Party. Whigs promoted the idea of the Federal government involving itself in areas not authorized by the Constitution. Whigs were more often than not, viewed as Federal supremacists. It should be noted here that when Lincoln was elected to Congress in the 1840s he was a Whig and a great admirer of Henry Clay. Lincoln heaped praise upon Clay and followed Clay's policies as president. What most modern historians don't like to tell folks is that Clay was a large slaveholder. Ironic is it not? Lincoln's political hero was a slaveholder!

As the slavery issue, especially the issue of allowing slaves into the newly acquired territories, became more heated Lincoln threw his lot in with the new Republican Party—this is the same Republican Party that many Southerners vote for today. The Republican Party that attracted radical socialists and communists into its ranks in the first few decades of its existence is also the party that today is held up as the party of limited government. Joseph Weydemeyer, who Marx declared to be "my good friend Joseph Weydemeyer" is one of many Marxists who helped establish the Republican Party, helped elect Lincoln as America's first Republican President, and became one of Lincoln's communist generals fighting against Southern independence. Oh look, another irony! The same Karl Marx who worked for the defeat of the Confederate States of America is the same Karl Marx who proclaimed that the South was fighting the war to defend and promote slavery. This is the same view of the War for Southern Independence that both modern major political parties and conservatives such a Rush Limbaugh, Bill O'Riley and Sean Hannity espouse. Now that is truly ironic! Conservatives parroting the words of Karl Marx.

Many people will argue about what was the true cause of the War for Southern Independence was but it was Marx who first said the South fought for slavery. He did this for one major reason—propaganda. Europe was mostly anti-slavery in sentiment and if Marx could convince Europeans that the South wanted only to promote slavery no European nation would recognize or otherwise give aid to the South. Marx was very successful. Yet when we ask a Radical Republican what the war was all about the answer is quite clear. In a speech promoting the idea of Lincoln as a non-Christian and a Freethinker, Colonel Robert Ingersoll of the 11th Indiana Cavalry tells us what the War was all about: "The great stumbling block, the great obstruction in Lincoln's way and in the way of thousands, was the old doctrine of State's Rights." Yes, State Sovereignty was the great stumbling block to the growth of big government and Federal supremacy. As long as REAL State's Rights existed, "we the people" at the state level could force the Federal government to abide by the Constitution. But without **REAL** State's Rights the Constitution becomes a thing of clay to be molded in whatever manner the Federal supremacists may desire. The governmental agent created by sovereign states has become the master not the servant of its creators!

So now we see the true nature of each type of republican: Jeffersonian republicans believe in a Federal government that can and MUST be forced to abide by a written constitution. Because the people at the local level are sovereign, they and they alone determine how they are to be governed, not Federal judges, Federal politicians, or Federal bureaucrats. The tools of REAL States' Rights are interposition, nullification, and secession. No wonder radical socialists, communists, Freethinkers, High Federalists and other advocates of Federal supremacy sought to defeat the South at any cost—*any cost was worth the defeat of the South if the old obstacle of States' Rights could be removed.* As if he was speaking for the entirety of his Federal supremacy comrades, Ralph Waldo Emerson stated, "If it cost ten years, and ten to recover the general prosperity, the destruction of the South is worth so much." It should be noted that while many people will tell us that Emerson hated the South because of slavery, he never expressed similar emotions about his family's role in the African-slave trade. Remember, his great grandfather, Cornelius Waldo, was an active slave-trader.

During the past few months, we have witnessed a resurgent call for limited government and State's Rights. Unfortunately, in post-Appomattox America, REAL State's Rights are dead. States' Rights died at the hands of the advocates of Federal supremacy, the archenemy of real republicanism.

Although we are looking at republicanism in the American context, that is, Jefferson republican vs. Lincoln republican, the roots of this struggle go all the way back to England before the Glorious Revolution. Life in England was grand if an individual had connections in the court of the King. The King could dispense large amounts of money and favors to his courtiers. The King routinely dispensed goodies such as royal monopolies, grants of land and titles. Of course, the hard-working folks, both common and noble who lived far away from the court of the King, you know out in the "fly-over" country of England, paid the King's taxes, which he then dispensed to the royal cronies at court leaving the folks out in the country with nothing but royal tyranny. This and other forms of mercantilism were good for the King and his courtiers but were oppressive to the people who lived away from London, out in the country. Thus, two opposing views of government arose in England, one believing that the King and his court were essential for promoting the economic well-being of the Kingdom and the other believing that the King's court was oppressive to the good and well-being of those living away from the court, and therefore, the country. This is very similar to what we see in America after independence. It is also stunningly similar to affairs in Washington today. The King's Court has been replaced by the Federal government.

In 1920 a German economist, Ludwig von Mises, pointed out, "The old colonial policy of Europe was mercantilistic, militaristic, and imperialistic." As Mises points out, it takes a strong central government to support a "mercantilistic, militaristic, and imperialistic" government. We should remember that as government grows, liberty shrinks. Your liberty and property are the life blood of big government. Let me repeat it one more time: Individual liberty and personal property IS the life blood of big government. Big government is a parasite and a parasite can kill its host.

The failures of the country element in England to protect the local people from an abusive central government were not lost on the leading Anti-Federalists in America. These early republicans understood that terms such as "divine right" and "parliamentary supremacy" would, *if not aggressively resisted,* be replaced by the terms "general welfare" and "federal supremacy." Understanding human nature, John Taylor of Caroline declared, "Tyranny is wonderfully ingenious in the art of inventing specious phrases to spread over its nefarious designs." Is this not an apt description of what we have come to know as "Obama-Care?"

If you are a Jeffersonian republican the question finally comes down to this: How do we in the words of John Taylor of Caroline, "aggressively resist" the efforts of the Federal supremacist? Jefferson and Madison in the Virginia and Kentucky Resolutions gave us clear and unequivocal directions on this subject. Only by using the tools of REAL States' Rights, that is, interposition, nullification, and secession can our agent, the Federal government, be compelled to abide by the limitations of the Constitution. Any other effort is nothing less than "a fool's errand!"

But here we run into another problem. Since Appomattox we do not have REAL States' Rights, we have States' Privileges. There is nothing under the sun that a State can do today that the Federal government cannot void at its will. A "Right" cannot be removed; whereas, a Privilege is exercised at the volition of the superior agent. Since Appomattox the Federal government is the superior agent in America. We should all recall the old, common-law adage:

"**A right without a remedy is a nullity.**" What remedy do Americans currently have when our rights reserved under the Constitution are abused, oppressed, and ignored by a supreme Federal government? In reality, under the current system of Federal supremacy we the people of the once sovereign states have no rights that the Federal government is required to recognize.

In his book, *Reclaiming Liberty,* Ron Kennedy demonstrated how for the past one hundred years the advocates of limited government have experienced one failure after another. Even in our lifetime we have witnessed the advocates of limited government (Jeffersonian republicans) taking over both houses of Congress and the White House. Yet has government decreased in power and taxing authority after these so-called victories? The answer is no. Government is much larger today than when President Clinton was forced to utter the phrase "the era of big government is dead." Why does government continue to get bigger even after so many conservative electoral victories? Even Mr. Limited Government himself, Ronald Regan, could not stop let alone turn back the growth of government. Why? The answer to this question should be obvious to any true Anti-Federalist or Jeffersonian Republican. With the loss of REAL States' Rights "we the people" no longer have the tools necessary to force the Federal government to abide by the Constitution. Until we reestablish in the **hearts and minds of our people** and in our Constitution that REAL States' Rights are a reality, we will never be able to control the modern-day Federal Supremacist regime regardless of whether the Federal regime is managed by Republicans or Democrats. Electing more Lincoln Republicans will not help—it did not help during the hay-day of Newt Gingrich or during the presidency of Ronald Regan—it will not help today. *Something else must be done.*

After the success of *The South Was Right,* Ron and I wrote *Why Not Freedom.* In this book we demonstrate just how tyrannical America has become due to the loss of REAL States' Rights. In both *Reclaiming Liberty* and *Why Not Freedom,* a proposed constitutional amendment is offered to force the Federal government to recognize the right of "we the people" to nullify un-Constitutional acts of the federal government and if necessary, secede from an abusive government. As John Locke pointed out, no man can be free if he does not possess a means of escaping tyranny. "We the people" must put the Federal government on notice that it must live by the Constitution or else. If we have in our hands the tools to compel the Federal government to abide by the Constitution and if we have the courage to use those tools, true Jeffersonian republicanism will return to American.

Ron and I still believe that the only way to regain the tools necessary to compel the Federal government to conduct itself according to the Constitution is by passing a constitutional amendment acknowledging the unalienable right of "we the people" of the sovereign state to nullify acts of the Federal government we judge to be unconstitutional.

We are now at that point in time which President Jefferson Davis spoke of when he stated, "The principle for which we contend is bound to reassert itself, but it may be at another time and in another form." Furthermore, as Vice President Stephens stated after the defeat of the South, the day will come when every American would understand that "the cause of the South is the cause of all." With all that is going on today, I believe that OUR time has, at last, come. Let us all do our duty in promoting the Cause of the South and one day we shall be free. Always remember, "If you can't leave, you are not free!" Endlessly singing "Glory, glory, halleluiah" and repeating "land of the free, home of the brave" will not change that reality! Let us be about the duty of promoting real American liberty—just like our Confederate forefathers. God bless you and our Southland.

Chapter IX

SCV: THE WELL-KEPT SECRET

GROWING UP IN THE 1950S in Mississippi my twin brother and I were admonished by our mother, "You don't have to tell everything you know" and "Everybody's business is nobody's business." Surely this was good advice for immature young boys but when it comes to defending the truth about Southern heritage and history, this is not a good rule to follow. Providing people with the truth is the most important job of every defender of the South. After all, we are in the business of letting folks hear the truth about the South. Unfortunately, when it comes to telling our side of the story, we of the SCV have done a good job of making our organization and point of view the "Well-Kept Secret." Let me give you a few examples of what I mean.

Recently I had the honor of attending the Pacific Northwest SCV Division Reunion in Nampa, Idaho. What an honor and pleasure it was to be given such a warm "Southern" welcome by our Confederate Compatriots in the Northwest! On my return flight from the Northwest, I was seated next to a gentleman in his mid-fifties who was returning home to Houston, Texas. During the flight we discussed why I had been in Idaho. I noticed a perplexed look on the face of my fellow passenger as I explained that I was speaking to members of the Sons of Confederate Veterans. He stated that he was amazed that such a group existed and that it would have members "way out there!" When I told him, I was Chief of Heritage Operations for the SCV and that the SCV was an international organization composed of a diverse group of men who were proud of their Confederate heritage, the gentleman looked at me as if I was just pulling a prank on him. He stated that his family had been in

Texas for many generations and he grew up and lived in the Houston, Texas, area but had never heard of the "Sons of the Confederacy." His response is not an isolated case.

In October I received from our Make Dixie Great Again website the following e-mail: "I heard your ad on Rush Limbaugh, it was a local ad. I am not sure if you are the ones I want to contact, but I believe history should never be exterminated. My ancestors fought in the Civil War for the Confederacy. I am not ashamed of this. I am proud that they stood up for their beliefs. I have absolutely nothing against persons of color. If this is what your organization supports, please contact me." The person sending this e-mail had no idea about the SCV but notice he stated his love for family and his family's history. Also notice, until he heard our Radio Free Dixie ad, he did not even know we existed—another person suffering from the SCV's "Well-Kept Secret." In January of this year, while being interviewed by a Yankee news crew in New Orleans at Lee Circle, a group of six New Orleans construction workers interrupted the interview by questioning the news crew on what was going on. When they were told by this Yankee news crew that Mr. Kennedy is explaining why Lee should not have been taken down, all six men jumped into the fray and gave one of the best defenses of General Lee I have ever heard. The Yankee news crew was shocked by their very bold and positive view of General Lee and asked the six men if they were members of the SCV. None were members of the SCV and only one said that he thought he had heard something about "that group." Again, more victims of the SCV's "Well-Kept Secret."

Before writing this edition of 'Forward the Colors,' I made an on-the-spot survey of a large group of Trump supporters attending a Trump Rally in Monroe, La. There were over 10,000 people from all parts of Louisiana and several Southern States at this rally. I randomly picked a dozen or so people and asked them these two questions: (1) Do you think America's traditional values and history are under attack by left-wing radicals? (2) Do you know what is the purpose of the Sons of Confederate Veterans? The first question got a 100% yes response. The second question, about 90% of the time, got the same perplexed and puzzled look that I have seen so many times before. Those who had at least heard of the SCV could not tell me what the SCV stood for other than "They like to dress up like

Rebels." I did meet one fellow SCV member in the crowd and saw at least two other men whom I know are supporters of the Cause of the South. Nevertheless, at that place there was a very large group of people who love our history and understand that our values are under attack, yet they do not quickly recognize who and what the SCV is all about. This impromptu survey speaks volumes about the SCV's "Well-Kept Secret."

When the average American conservative, who loves our history and feels like traditional American values are under attack, cannot identify the SCV and what the SCV is promoting—our heritage is in major danger! How do you think this impacts the political establishment? If our SCV "footprint" is so small in our communities as to go unrecognized by these conservative Americans, how can you expect the political establishment to recognize and/or fear us? Remember it is the political establishment who kowtow to anti-American radical leftists. When push comes to shove, who do you think the political establishment will fearfully bend to? Will they kowtow to those who have clout or to those whom no one even recognizes? Confederate monuments have been removed, Confederate flags banned and/or excluded from parades, not by Federal agents from Washington but by cowardly local politicians of both political parties. Politicians are very astute at evaluating the cost and consequences of any policy or procedure they support or oppose. Very often the major factor in determining their support or opposition to a policy or procedure is based upon this cost/benefit analysis. If these politicians (in older days they would have been called "scalawags") hear of all the efforts and support the left-wing radicals have and hardly even know the defenders of the South even exists, guess whose agenda will receive the support of the establishment. The SCV MUST increase its social footprint in our communities or the game is up! How shall we convert the SCV from a well-kept secret to a well-known organization? There is some good news about that process.

Recently the Make Dixie Great Again website received an e-mail from a supporter in Brazil. After viewing one of our Make Dixie Great Again videos on our You Tube channel, he sent us this message: "Your cousins from Brazil share the Respect, the Love and the Heritage. God bless you all." This supporter of Dixie in Brazil understands that our message is a good and wholesome message and that it needs to be shared with his neighbors. He has taken the time to view our videos and pass them on to others—he is not keeping this a secret! What is true for our compatriot in Brazil is even more true for us here in the once free and prosperous Confederate States of America. We need to get busy and utilize the tools (videos, radio ads, handouts, articles) made available on the Make Dixie Great Again website and share them with friends on social media and the general public. Individuals or local SCV camps should purchase time on local radio stations and run our pro-South SCV ads, purchase copies of the 'Southern Defender' and give them out at fairs, living histories, camp events, and leave a few copies at every waiting room in your community. These are just a few things that with very minimal effort or expense every SCV camp can participate in and thereby increase the SCV's community footprint. As our footprint increases, the establishment at large will begin to notice and most importantly, that great mass of potential supporters will KNOW (as noted in previous articles in this magazine, our supporters compose upwards of 70% of Southerners) who we are and become *active* supporters and eventually members of the SCV. As Commander Gramling has stated, "We must take back the narrative." The "narrative" has been stolen from us but now, like never before, we have a real chance to "Take back the Narrative!" It all depends upon you. Join the Confederate Legion! Remember that 90% of your donation/membership fees are used to buy and or distribute positive pro-South ads, videos, and articles. We can win but we must act now and do so with victory as our ultimate goal! Deo Vindice.

GOING ON THE OFFENSE: ATTACK-ATTACK-ATTACK

The following article was written and published in an effort to inform and inspire members of the SCV and other such Southern Rights organizations to fight smart. The Cause of the South cannot be defended and our enemies defeated by allowing the neo-Marxists to have and hold a monopoly on information about the Southern Cause. As noted in the following article, we must face a 21st century enemy with 21st century weapons and tactics.

As is explained in the January/February 2020 issue of the *Confederate Veteran* magazine, 'Forward the Colors,' the SCV is a well-kept secret. At times like this the SCV needs to be known as an active and therefore very strong defender of Southern Rights. Unfortunately, as a group founded in the 19th century and maturing as an organization in the 20th century, we tend to fight our enemies with 19th and 20th century weapons and tactics. Regrettably, our enemies are using 21st century weapons and tactics. Think of it like this: If the most powerful WWII (20th century) military force was attacked by a very small but well equipped 21st century military force the 20th century force would be defeated—the same is true for the SCV and its promotion and defense of Southern heritage.

The relentless attack by the leftist political/social establishment in Virginia is a perfect example of why the SCV must have a better system of defending *and* promoting our heritage. Consider these past relentless attacks upon our heritage/history: Charleston, Charlottesville, and New Orleans. Notice how fast our enemies can respond to these events and therefore capture the attention of the majority of Americans for their anti-South narrative. Now consider how long it took and even now takes the SCV to respond. In WWII as the German Blitzkrieg was over-running France, the French military headquarters did not even have wireless or telephone connection with its field commanders—headquarters was still using WWI style runners with written messages for communications—the French military did not keep up with technology, the Germans did. This is the state of affairs today as we witness a continuation of the destruction of Southern heritage.

This is not a criticism of previous SCV leaders. They had to work with the tools that they had at the time. What the SCV needs to do is to update its ability to respond to our enemies. This cannot be done by volunteers. The Confederate Legion's ability to respond to any attack is hampered by lack of manpower and resources. What is needed is a full-time department at headquarters that will be responsible for reaching out to SCV Divisions, Camps, and members as soon as an "incident" or attack takes place and give those Division, Camps, and members a working plan of action to counter the attack upon our history/heritage. This new full-time department should also daily be working to place SCV information on radio, print media, and social media. At this time, those of us working in the Confederate Legion are attempting to do all of this and more on a volunteer basis. The little good we are seeing now with volunteers (4-5 people) can be multiplied a hundred times with a full-time individual. Also, the benefit of a quick and timely response to the news and social media will give us a chance to put our narrative before the public quickly and therefore help stem the tide of anti-South bigotry.

If we do not give new SCV leaders the tools to fight our enemies in a 21st century method, the SCV and our Southern Heritage is as doomed as the French military facing the German Blitzkrieg. We can win this fight but we must fight smart—the question is, "Does the SCV have the will to jump into a 21st century fight?"

The preceding is the opinion of Walter D. Kennedy, Chief of Heritage Operations and has not been endorsed by anyone other than his twin brother!

Chapter X

ROBERT E. LEE:
TRAITOR AND DEFENDER OF SLAVERY?

RECENTLY A PHD (DOCTORAL) CANDIDATE at Boston College published an article in which he attempts to prove that General Robert E. Lee was a notorious American traitor and defender of slavery. According to his article, which was picked up and widely circulated, not only was Lee second only to Benedict Arnold on the "treason scale" but Lee was also a vigorous defender of slavery. Of course, we all should recognize this attack upon General Lee is merely a slight-of-hand attack upon all Southerners who would be so audacious as to resist the Yankee's not-so-loving embrace.

Even an abbreviated look at the charge of treason against Lee will quickly and completely expose this Yankee's absurd charge as a puerile and foolish attempt at building oneself up by attacking a great man. In announcing that Lee was a traitor, the author states that as a United States Army officer, Lee had taken an oath to "defend and protect the Constitution of the United States." Since Lee resigned his commission and join "a rebel army based in Virginia," this, according to our PhD candidate, was proof positive of Lee's treason. One would think that a PhD candidate would understand that Lee's oath was to the Constitution and not to the government, president, or union. Nowhere in the Constitution is the Federal government granted the right to invade a state of the union unless said action is requested by the duly elected government of that state, (Article IV, Section IV). As Alexander Hamilton (*Federalists Paper No. 33*) and James Madison (*Federalist Paper No. 45*) both noted, any action taken by the Federal government that was not PURSUANT to the Constitution was null and void. Lincoln's call for an army to invade sovereign states to enforce un-Constitutional laws could only be answered by those who were willing to turn their back upon the Constitution—the highest form of treason. It would make just as much sense to argue for the use of rape to defend virginity as to argue for using un-Constitutional actions to defend the Constitution! The Doctoral Candidate's statement that Lee "joined a rebel army" is somewhat ironic. Has this "educated" man ever read or studied the history of the Minute Men of Massachusetts? When defending their "Rights of Englishmen" against English tyranny, the Minute Men of Massachusetts were also slandered by the defenders of big government as "joining a rebel army."

The Boston Doctoral Candidate's bashing of Lee continues with the well-established myth of Lee, and therefore the South, fighting for slavery. This charge is also supported by a host of sophomoric arguments that borders on the juvenile. In his article the candidate states that since Lee was an officer in the Confederate government which did not allow a state to secede, nor limit or end slavery, he was supporting slavery and rejecting secession. Here is his rational: The Confederate Constitution denied the states of the Confederacy the right to secede and to limit or eliminate slavery. This PhD candidate is merely repeating the ideas and propaganda of Karl Marx who stated, "The war of the Southern Confederacy is...a war of conquest for the extension and perpetuation of slavery." Nowhere in the Constitution of the Confederate States of America is there a prohibition against any state of the Confederacy from "limiting or elimination" of slavery. What the Confederate Constitution does is to prohibit the central government from sticking its nose into the business of the states. This concept that the issue of slavery must be solved by the people of the states and not the central government is not strictly a Southern concept. It was none other than Oliver Ellsworth of Connecticut who in 1787 declared, "The morality or wisdom of slavery are considerations belonging to the States...the States are the best judges of their particular interests." Our Boston detractor seems to have overlooked several other important points while condemning Lee and the South: Slavery has a longer history in Massachusetts than Georgia by 5 years and Massachusetts has a 72-years-longer history of slavery than Alabama or Mississippi; he forgot that more slaves were given their freedom by Southerners than any people in the civilized world; and he overlooked the fact that it was Southerners who fought against Yankee slave traders to eliminate the African slave trade. One particularly infuriating myth our not-so-well-educated PhD candidate asserted was that before the election of Lincoln, "wealthy white plantation owners in the South...took over the United States government." This remark was intended to demonstrate that the so-called "slave power" of the South was trying to enforce slavery all across America. Our sophomoric detractor missed one very important point: wealthy plantation owners were more likely to be members of the Whig Party. The most prominent member of that party was Abraham Lincoln's idol and hero, Henry Clay. Clay was a wealthy slave holder. When Lincoln first announced his move into politics, he did so by proclaiming himself to be a "Henry Clay Whig." At Clay's death, Lincoln gave a memorial speech praising Clay but never once did Lincoln condemn Clay the slave holder. Most Whigs in the South opposed secession and had to be pressured and otherwise forced into supporting secession. Secession was anything but a "slave-holders" idea or effort. As for the idea that the Confederate Constitution denied to the States the right to secede, one only has to look at the preamble of that document which states: "We the people of the Confederate States, each State acting in its sovereign and independent character... ." A "sovereign and independent" State has every right to accede or secede at its own will, enough said!

In a final assault upon reason and correct history, our deluded Boston PhD candidate stated that the Confederate Constitution was a "cheap imitation of the United States Constitution." He maintains that the Confederate Constitution removed all language that promoted the American Constitutional values of "equality, freedom, and justice." Our Bostonian candidate must have forgotten that in 1776 slavery existed in ALL thirteen states and those states that had few slaves were the very ones promoting and enriching themselves via the nefarious African slave trade. Even within white society, there was no vaunted "equality." Our founding fathers understood that no one was born with the right to govern others. The only form of equality that American society embraced was an anti-hereditary aristocracy. Our founding fathers were republican in spirit not Marxist. The word "freedom" only appears in the Bill of Rights which was added to the Constitution by the action of the Anti-Federalists who were advocates of State Sovereignty. Within the Confederate Constitution every right that is protected in the U. S. Bill of Rights is enumerated and protected by the Confederate Constitution—thus, the same "justice" is acknowledged by both the Confederate and the U. S. Constitution.

There is a very good reason to study the words and actions of our enemies who seek our ultimate and total destruction. Most readers of the *Confederate Veteran Magazine* will dismiss out of hand the assertions of this Bostonian detractor of Lee and the South. That is good but that is also bad! If we do not "take back the narrative" and give the Southern view of Lee and the South, only the voice of our detractors will be heard. Too often we hear such nonsense as what this PhD candidate spews forth and, knowing the truth, just move on. Yet, there is a generation of young Southerners who will not understand the truth about our noble heritage if we don't get busy and tell "the rest of the story." This is why Commander Grambling established the Southern Victory Campaign. By organizing our members and camps into fighting units, we can "take back the narrative." For the past eighteen months the Confederate Legion has been taking our message to the people of the South and attempting to increase the SCV's footprint across the diverse population of the South.

The following list is not an exhaustive list of what we have been doing in our efforts to "take back the narrative" but it will give our SCV members an idea of what the Heritage Operations Committee has been able to accomplish.

1. Established a professional studio for making pro-South videos.
2. Secured website domain names and built SCV Confederate Legion website, Make Dixie Great Again.
3. Wrote and recorded 14 videos about issues related to Southern history and heritage.
4. Produced and ran sixteen 'Commander's Comment' videos. Visit the MDGA website each month to view that month's Commander's Comment video.

5. Established Make Dixie Great Again Facebook account and kept it current.
6. Ran six "Special Ops" promoting events that relate to Southern heritage.
7. Wrote and professionally taped more than a dozen one-minute, pro-South radio ads.
8. Bought and placed over $20,000.00 in radio ads for Radio Free Dixie, all of which point people to our MDGA website.
9. Sent letters to elected officials about why they need to support Southern history and heritage.
10. Created and offered to camps sample letters to be sent to elected officials, churches, ministers, civic and veteran organizations. These letters serve two purposes: Inform the general public about who we are and that we are active in the local community, and also inform the political establishment that we are a power to be reckoned with.
11. Created and offered for use by local camps the *'Southern Defender.'* The *'Southern Defender'* is a four-page, multi-color flyer suitable for insertion in local newspapers, given out at fairs, living history events, gun shows, or just left in every waiting room in the South! If every SCV camp would buy fifty of these inserts (price, 29 to 39 cents each) and put them in waiting rooms in their community every two months, the SCV could enlighten and inform over 260,000 people each year. With this and other such actions, the SCV would no longer be a well-kept secret but a viable force to be dealt with.
12. Hosted on the MDGA website and Facebook four 90 second recruitment videos provided by Lt. Commander-in-Chief, Larry McCluney, Jr.

The preceding is just some of the work the Confederate Legion has been doing to promote and defend our heritage. This along with the various efforts by our legal staff are making a difference but it is no good unless SCV members and local camps support our effort. If you are not a member of the Confederate Legion and if your camp is not actively supporting these efforts described herein, please join now and let's take back the narrative. Remember, if we fail to give a vigorous and aggressive response when the neo-Marxist enemies attack our heritage, then Southern heritage will surely die with us. Seeing the obstacles before us, some have given up and become defeated but we should always remember that "Only those who accept defeat are defeated." I, like most of you, refuse to accept defeat because I understand that as long as one person is willing to light his candle of freedom, the Cause of the South will yet enlighten a darkened World. Deo Vindice!

A NAME DOES REVEAL A TRUTH

The irony of turning Robert E. Lee into an American traitor while celebrating Abraham Lincoln is especially frustrating when one understands that Marxist, Radical Socialists and even Adolf Hitler were admirers of Lincoln. Who is the real traitor to the original America, the man who is admired by Communists and Nazis (Lincoln) or the defender of the America given to us by our Founding Fathers? This article points out just who should be ostracized and who should be admired.

As any parent will tell you, naming a child can be a very stressful and important part of parenting. Indeed, the first thing we usually learn about a person is his name. What is true in the life of a family is just as true in the political life of a nation. Just after the outbreak of the Spanish Civil War, circa 1936, a small group of American leftists, i.e., communists, socialists, and other "progressives," established what was to become known as "The Lincoln Brigade."

The Lincoln Brigade consisted of American volunteers who served in Spain supporting the Marxist government. The Marxist Spanish government was fighting against General Francisco Franco, leader of the Fascist element in Spain. It should be obvious that both sides of this civil war were socialist and were advocates of big government. Regardless of which side won the war, big government was the victor and individual liberty the loser.

As has been demonstrated in *Lincoln's Marxists* and *Lincoln Uber Alles*, early American socialists and communists had a great affinity for Abraham Lincoln. With their long history of love for Lincoln is it any wonder that radical leftists in 1936 adopted the name of "Lincoln" for the brigade of volunteers? To this day, the supporters and admirers of The Lincoln Brigade support all the trendy left-wing ideas and movements that promote big government. Lincoln's support by Marxists and socialists in the 1860s was transformed in the 1930s into Marxists and socialists using Lincoln's name to advance their left-wing agenda. Although The Lincoln Brigade fought against Fascists and Hitler in the Spanish Civil War, Adolf Hitler embraced the philosophy of Lincoln as it relates to State's Rights and national sovereignty. Historically, it seems that all Fascists, Marxists, and Nazis adored Lincoln.

In his book, *Mein Kampf*, Hitler virtually quotes Lincoln in his defense of building a strong "indivisible" German nation. In 1861 Lincoln proclaimed that the States of the American Union had never been "sovereign." In speaking of the American Union in his book, Hitler states: "Originally these states did not and could not possess sovereign rights of their own." In defense of his invasion of the States of the American Union, Lincoln stated that it was the Union that had created the States "*such as they are.*" In *Mein Kampf* Hitler asserts that the States of the American Union could not be sovereign because "... it was the Union that created most of these *so-called states.*" In his book Hitler, like Lincoln, makes it clear that he is an advocate of a strong, indivisible republic. Hitler was so much opposed to the idea of secession that he and his Nazi followers launched their first attempt to take over a German state to prevent its secession from the German Federal Republic. Obviously, Hitler in 1923 had no more hesitation at using military force to prevent a people from exercising their right of self-determination than Lincoln did in 1861.

In the Declaration of Independence self-government is announced in the words, "Government by the consent of the governed." It seems that neither Lincoln nor Hitler approved of that famous declaration. After the defeat of Nazism in 1945 an American Veteran of World War II established the American Nazi Party. The name of that American, who was a distinguished American Veteran of both World War Two and the Korean War, was George Lincoln Rockwell. Rockwell was born in Central Illinois, not far from where Lincoln got his start in politics, and educated at Brown University in Providence, Rhode Island. It should be noted that Brown University was named in honor of an infamous Yankee slave-trader. Once again, we see that the name of Lincoln is associated with those elements that advocate big government.

Big government is the antithesis of individual liberty. Also in the American context, big government is THE enemy of limited government, that is, States' Rights. Whether one is speaking of Marx, Engels, Hitler, or Lincoln, the title of "big government advocate" is a perfect fit. Unfortunately, most "conservative" commentators: Levine, Beck, Hannity or any number of such right-wing talking heads view Lincoln as a defender of limited government. Yet, it was Lincoln who drew the support of radical socialists Karl Marx and

Fredrick Engels during the so-called "Civil War." After Lincoln's death it was radical socialists, communists and Nazis who identified with Lincoln. Hitler's aggressive use of force to build and maintain his "perpetual" Union is little different than Lincoln's policy of invasion and conquest. When will conservative commentators face the truth about Lincoln, America's number one Fascist? Perhaps we should simply refer to Lincoln as "America's Fascist Founding Father!" We should also proudly proclaim to the world that our Confederate Fathers were defending the REAL America!

Chapter XI

ANTI-SOUTH BIGOTRY CONTINUES

I AM SURE THE READERS of the *Confederate Veteran* magazine are not shocked by the fact that the false narrative about the South is continuing. What is shocking is the ability of these anti-South bigots to proclaim the most absurd falsehoods without ever being questioned of their validity. For example, recently the Stephen D. Lee Institute Symposium in Raleigh, NC, was condemned by radical leftists as being a "white-supremist" gathering. This false narrative was picked up and published by the *Huffington Post*, thereby furthering the "hate the South" agenda of the radical left and politically correct society.

In a truly free and open society, news reporters and commentators would engage in a fair and complete investigation of the Symposium to determine the validity of the white-supremist charge. An impartial investigation would have shown that there were five lectures on Southern history, culture, and government without any "white-supremist" statement being made. All five speakers were Ph.D., level individuals with hundreds of academic articles and books published by these men. Simply put, no-one on the left cares to tell our side of the story.

To add insult to injury, recently the Commandant of the Marine Corps, General David B. Berger, stated that all Confederate Flags would be prohibited on any Marine Base or area. In response to his anti-Confederate action, I wrote General Berger the following letter:

March 15, 2020
General David H. Berger
Commandant of the Marine Corps
Headquarters, US Marine Corps
3000 Marine Corps, Pentagon
Washington, DC 20350-3000

Dear Sir,

As the father of a U. S. Marine and the great-grandson of a Confederate veteran, I am very distressed with your recent attack upon my family's heritage. I am hopeful that said attack was un-intentional but un-intentional or not, I am greatly offended. My son's maternal grandfather was a WWII Marine who witnessed the famous raising of the flag on Mt. Suribachi and he too was a descendent of a Confederate veteran.

On a more personal note, I recently took part in the funeral of my elder brother, Alton Kennedy. Draped over his casket was a U. S. Flag. Alton was a member of the famous 31st U.S. Army Infantry Division, AKA, the Dixie Division. My brother's grave is located not 30 feet from the grave of John Wesley Kennedy, Co. F, 38th Mississippi Volunteer Infantry, C.S.A; our great-grandfather. Please understand that for a very large number of Southerners, when you attack the Confederate Flag, you are attacking our family. You recently stated that your anti-Confederate action was an effort to remove "Things that divide us." How can insulting the families of thousands of patriotic Americans promote that effort? May I remind you that Southerners are much more likely to serve our nation than Northerners. While the South is over-represented in the military by 20%, people from the Northeast are under-represented by 20%. I am sure those Southerners who hit the black sands of Iwo Jima were not doing so in order for their family to be insulted and defamed by the very Marine Corps and nation that they were serving.

The misuse of symbols is disheartening but the misuse of the symbol and not the symbol is what should come under examination and correction. I have attached a photo of a large KKK rally held in Washington, DC. Please note that this photo is full of white-robed Klansmen carrying *not* Confederate Flags but United States Flags. The most common flag associated with any Klan rally is the United

States Flag and not the Confederate Flag. With that fact in mind, why are you displaying such contempt for the Confederate Flag? I have also attached a photo of the slave ship, 'Nightingale." Please note that as in the case of most American slave ships, there is a U.S. Flag and not a Confederate Flag flying from the slave-ship. Once again, I must point out that it is the misuse of symbols and not the symbols that is at fault. Again, I will ask, why do you choose to attack the Confederate Flag? Honorable Southerners are equally insulted when hate-groups use our flags, U.S. or Confederate, to promote bigotry but please, "don't throw out the baby with the bathwater!" It is the misuse that must be corrected—censoring flags, U.S. or Confederate, is not the answer.

When viewing actions such as yours, many people question if Southerners are now being treated as conquered people who no longer possess the right to have pride in their family. Are Southerners now officially recognized as second-class citizens in America? What other group of American citizens are denied the right to express pride in their heritage? Sadly, sir, the answer is that only the children of the conquered nation, The Confederate States of America, are treated thusly. And yet, it is from the Confederate veterans that some of America's most famous military leaders (many of whom were Marines) have descended.

I am a proud member of the Sons of Confederate Veterans (SCV) and hold the office of Chief of Heritage Operations. The gentleman who preceded me in this office was a Marine and a member of the General Executive Council of the SCV, which is the governing body of the SCV. This Council is composed of no less than three Marines which is 20% of the Council. All other branches of the U.S. military service are also represented and those without military service have children and/or grandchildren in America's military service. The SCV is a patriotic, benevolent, and historical organization and as such, respectfully request that you remove *not the symbol* but the *misuse of the symbol* of our Confederate Veterans. Please note that our organization fully embraces the diversity of the South and the Confederate military. We are proud of the service of all Southerners during the War for Southern Independence and therefore our membership reflects all ethnic groups in the South, black, red, brown, and white, as well as all religious groups of the South. The

SCV promotes real diversity and tolerance. Our hope is that this policy will be followed by the United States Marine Corps—by showing tolerance for Confederate heritage.

Walter D. Kennedy

Chief of Heritage Operations, SCV

cc: Louisiana Congressional and Senatorial delegation

President Donald Trump

Mark Esper, Secretary of Defense

We Southerners can be proud of the spirit of our forefathers who courageously stood up to those who would trample our Rights. That spirit lives today. For example, the Southern city of Fayetteville, NC, population of 205,000, provides twice the number of military servicemen that Manhattan, NY, population of 1.6 million! The truth of the matter is that the U. S. military speaks with a Southern accent.

As pointed out in the beginning of this article, no one will give our side of this story. Therefore, we must make every effort to tell the truth about our history and heritage or surely that "little upon which we now barely exist will be taken from us." Please notice that I cc'd a copy of my letter to my Louisiana delegation in Washington as well as to the President and Secretary of Defense. You can do the same and let's put the pressure on the liberal establishment. Also, join us by enlisting in the Confederate Legion. Visit us at: makedixiegreatagain.com Deo Vindice.

A SHOCKING WAKE-UP CALL

This article/incident occurred approximately six months before Paul Gramling, Jr. was elected Commander-in-Chief of the Sons of Confederate Veterans. Incidents such as this prompted Gramling to ask the Kennedy Twins to help him put together an SCV Southern Victory Campaign that would "take back the narrative" from the neo-Marxists who were on their way of complete destruction of all things Southern.

After being away from home for 68 years, on April 21, 2018 a 19-year-old MIA soldier from the Korean War was laid to rest in a small rural cemetery in North Central Louisiana. In order to receive the remains properly, the local community went to great pains to clean and beautify their cemetery. Understanding that a Confederate Veteran was buried in that cemetery I drove there the day before the service to inspect the marker for Pvt. Chris Bayles, Co K, 31st Louisiana Regt., C.S.A.

It's not often that those of us who regularly promote and defend the South need to have a "wake-up" call. But even the best defenders of the Southern Cause can be shocked by just how deeply rampant anti-South propaganda has penetrated our society. But, at this small rural cemetery, I was put on notice about the pervasiveness of anti-South propaganda. Now first let me remind everyone that this cemetery is in a very rural area of North Central Louisiana far removed from anything resembling a city. While taking photos of the Confederate Veteran's grave a lady, dressed and looking more like a jaded grounds keeper but who turned out to be the chairperson of the local cemetery committee, inquired about my presence in the cemetery. I was introduced to this lady by a mutual friend who happened to be in the cemetery at that time and assured the lady I was harmless. I informed the lady that I was checking on the status of the Confederate Veterans' graves in local cemeteries. I informed her that I was a member of the Sons of Confederate Veterans and that the SCV was interested in keeping a record of all Confederate Veterans' graves and seeing to it that their markers are maintained. At which point the lady chairperson somewhat aggressively asked why I was not doing that for WWII veterans. I again politely informed her that I was with the SCV and not the VFW. During our conversation the fact that the SCV also places Confederate Flags on these graves came up. Straightening herself up in her most commanding position, she informed me that "most people find that flag offensive." In an equal if not greater commanding voice I informed this lady that she was misinformed. As I explained it, yes there were some who did not like the Confederate Flag but that Americans in general and Southerners in particular have only positive feelings about that flag and the South.

Here is the point I wish to make about this incident. *We are losing!* If a woman from the hills of very rural Louisiana has been tainted with liberal lies and Yankee propaganda to the point she does not respect and honor Confederate Veterans or their flag, how much longer can we expect to have anyone, surely not a majority, who will stand with us? This lady was not born hating the South. Nevertheless, if we don't give her a reason to love the South and a reason to defend the honor of the Confederate Veterans, she will be pushed by liberal lies and Yankee propaganda to the point of at best, being embarrassed by the South, or at worst, hating the South.

It's easy to condemn this lady for her ill-spoken words but in reality her mis-information about the South are not solely her fault. The fact is that those of us who should be speaking for those Confederate Veterans have failed in our responsibility to "vindicate the Cause." In other words, it is *our* fault that she has not heard our narrative about our noble ancestors! She is daily inundated with anti-South messages from all forms of media, schools, and, sadly, left-leaning ministers. Someone has to tell "the rest of the story" and if not us, who? It is at this point fellow compatriots that we of the SCV have been a near total failure. Unless we place positive pro-South information before this lady and all of the citizens of the South, within ten years no Confederate monuments or flags will be allowed to be displayed *even on private property*. If we miss this wake-up call, we will miss the last chance to turn this struggle around and go on the march to final victory as we "Vindicate the Cause for which they fought." We (SCV) must put into place an information system that will cause Southerners to be proud of their heritage, and question and refute this avalanche of Yankee inspired lies.

On a good note, the g-g-granddaughter of the Confederate Veteran buried in the cemetery was the individual who initially introduced me to the "lady" chairperson. She knew all about Pvt. Bayles's Confederate service and politely informed me that I could place a Confederate Flag at her ancestor's grave anytime I desired. The point is gentlemen, we must support with positive information those who still hold true to the Cause of the South and make those who have imbibed in the left-wing, anti-South propaganda question and finally reject these attacks upon the South.

Paul Gramling has proposed just such a plan to go on the offensive if he is elected our next Commander-in-Chief. Nothing like this has been tried or even suggested by the leadership of the SCV in the 33 years that I have been a member. It's time to take the fight for our Southern heritage to all Southerners so we can save what we still have and take back that which has been taken from us.

Chapter XII

SCV and FIGHTING HATE

IN MODERN AMERICA there are at least three different views of the South as it relates to race and history. The most extreme view of the South is espoused by a group known as Black Lives Matter (BLM). According to BLM, those American States that composed the Confederate States of America, are inherently racist and evil. According to BLM, Southern racism runs so deep in the nature and composition of Southerners that the South must be destroyed. The destruction BLM activists are calling for is similar to what Nazis called for as they took control of Germany, or in a more modern context, what ISIS and Taliban extremists pursue. This attack upon various aspects of American culture is often referred to as "cancel culture," or more generally, "cultural genocide." What BLM activists are attempting to do is "cancel" all knowledge of the South that is out of keeping with their narrative of a hate-filled, evil, and racist South. An Irish Confederate Officer, Patrick Cleburne, warned that if the South lost its war for independence, Yankees would write and enforce the "official" history of the South. General Cleburne's warning has come true in the form of BLM, an anti-South media, and a government that offers cover and support for BLM misinformation.

If only BLM radicals were engaged in this attempt of cultural cleansing (cancel cultural) their ignoble campaign would quickly fail. Unfortunately, another group of anti-South bigots give tacit or implied support to BLM's campaign of anti-South, cultural genocide. While decrying the wanton and illegal destruction of Confederate memorials for Confederate heroes, these Americans fully agree with the BLM's false charge of Southern and/or Confederate inherent racism. This group of Americans control all major media and educational outlets. Using their control of media and education, they prevent or seriously limit access to these outlets for the traditional Southern view of the War for Southern Independence as well as the nature of race relations in both the Old South and the modern-day South. Very simply stated, the Southern view of its history and heritage suffers censorship via exclusion. This is the very thing Irish Confederate General Cleburne warned the South would happen. Having the Southern view of its history, heritage, and culture excluded from the marketplace of ideas makes it very easy for BLM to push its false narrative about the South.

The Sons of Confederate Veterans (SCV) has begun an effort to provide the general public a more factually accurate and complete story about the Confederate States of America and the South. The SCV was organized in 1896 to assist the then ageing Confederate Veterans, their widows, and their orphans. In 1906 General Stephen D. Lee, C.S.A., requested that the SCV advance the true history of the South and the truth about the Confederate States of America as well as its struggle to be free of Northern, Yankee domination. General Lee also requested that the Sons of Confederate Veterans work to "vindicate the Cause for which we fought."

With the increasingly slanderous and false attacks upon the South's history and culture, the SCV launched an effort to "take back the narrative." Since the Southern view of its history is denied a hearing in the normal media outlets, the SCV has begun using videos, radio ads, and print material to give the general public the truth about the War for Southern Independence, incorrectly labeled a "Civil War" by Yankees, and the truth about race and liberty in the South. This effort is centered around its new website, Make Dixie Great Again, www.makedixiegreatagain.org

The South's enemies eagerly condemn the South as the "home of slavery and racism." Yet, as is demonstrated in the many SCV videos and articles, this BLM charge is totally false. For example, slavery existed for 70 years longer in the Northern (Yankee) State of Massachusetts than in the Southern State of Mississippi (a Confederate State). A very similar comparison can be made between the Yankee State of New York and the Southern State of Alabama but still BLM and their deluded supporters condemn the South for

America's history of slavery. It is seldom acknowledged but it was the English colonies of the Southern portion of the United States that first protested against the nefarious African slave trade while the Northern colonies reaped huge profits from that same slave trade. From the earliest days of colonial America through the antebellum area prior to the War, it was the South which freed, at its own expense, more enslaved people than any nation on earth. It was the South which led the way in the formation of and membership in abolition societies. The truth is that the South inherited the system of African slavery and was well on the way of eliminating slavery when the United States invaded, conquered and occupied the South. Although the issue of ending slavery is used by the conquers of the South to justify their naked aggression and conquest of the Confederate States of America, the real reason for said aggression and conquest was the protection of Yankee profits.

When looking at the issue of slavery it should be remembered that slavery is not a Black vs White nor a North vs South issue. Slavery is a universal plague upon mankind. Every race has been enslaved and has been enslavers of their fellow man. Skin color is not the cause of slavery.

The idea that the South is the home of racism and the mistreatment of Black people in America is another false narrative pushed by BLM. The SCV offers the public a counter view that too often goes untold. Diversity is praised by most people in the United States but unknown to most people is the fact that the land and naval forces of the Confederate States of America were the most diverse military force in the nineteenth century. This diversity is reflected in the membership of the SCV. An example of Confederate diversity is displayed by the numerous African Americans, slave and free, who served in the Confederate military. Men such as Levy Carnine, a slave who became a Confederate hero, who not only fought for the South during the War but after the War became a faithful member of the United Confederate Veterans organization. When Levy died, his fellow Confederate veterans made sure he was buried alongside his fellow "white" Confederate Veterans. They were side by side during the War, after the War, and in death. The first Native American General officer in any American military force was Confederate General Stand Waite. The Confederate Army and Navy also enlisted numerous Hispanic

Americans both as officers and enlisted men. This history of diversity destroys the BLM false narrative of a hate-fill racist South.

The warm and cordial relationship between white and black Southerners prior to the War for Southern Independence was noted by many foreign travelers. Touring the South before the War, Frenchman Alex de Tocqueville, noted this warm relationship between the races in the South. Reflecting upon the South and race relations, Tocqueville noted, "In the South the Negros are less carefully kept apart, the Whites consent to intermix with Blacks." Tocqueville also noted that the "prejudice of race in much higher in the North than in the South." Tocqueville's statement is a representative sample of the hundreds of such examples, both American and foreign, who express the view that the BLM narrative of a hate-filled South is a false narrative.

After the defeat and occupation of the Confederate States of America by the United States, former Confederate General Robert E. Lee noted that with the defeat of the Confederate States of America by the victorious Yankees, America would become "aggressive abroad and despotic at home." General Lee understood that after their victory, Yankees would destroy States' Rights which served as a barrier to the growth of a national and international "aggressive abroad and despotic at home" United States. With the destruction of States' Rights, the path was open for the growth of an all-powerful government which Northerners would use to advance their profits at the expense of their conquered people. The traditional South fought for a small government that would not be aggressive abroad or despotic at home. This was the real purpose of States' Rights, that is, a means to keep the Federal government under the control of the people. This is the true reason that compelled the vast majority of non-slave holders of the South to join in the struggle for Southern independence. The SCV will continue to promote the truth about the Confederate States of America and the heritage of the South. The SCV will also continue to pursue General Stephen D. Lee's request made to the Sons of Confederate Veterans to, "vindicate the Cause for which we fought." Their fight is our fight; thus, we struggle against the false narrative of the BLM.

Chapter XIII

MAKING HISTORY vs REGRETTING HISTORY

HOW MANY TIMES have we Southerners discussed how if one or two events had ended differently, "we would have won the War!" I once heard several men discussing how victory for Southern independence could have been secured at First Manassas if we could have advanced on to Washington. The discussion was deep and filled with emotion until a very wise man interrupted our conversation with this profound statement: "Boys, you can't change history; why don't we get busy and MAKE HISTORY?"

He was right in the sense that "what is done, is done." But the stage of history is open for anyone who is willing to step-up and begin the process of making history. In today's world our neo-Marxist adversaries busy themselves with promoting a false narrative (fake history) about Southern history. These neo-Marxist ideologues are aided and supported by both left-wing and right-wing educators, media personalities, ministers, and quasi-historians. Recently while watching a History Channel program on *Weapons that Changed History*, I was informed by the commentator that the "Civil War" happened when the North sought to end slavery and the South fought to keep slavery alive. This statement is equally false and out of place. Nevertheless, this neo-Marxist sycophant felt compelled to "educate," more correctly "propagandize," the American public on his fake-history view of the War for Southern Independence. Just to keep the record straight, please remember that the Republican Party's fourth plank of its 1860 platform (the one Lincoln ran on) guaranteed the protection of slavery "where it now exists." Before his inauguration as president, Lincoln assured the South that slavery would be as safe under his administration as it was "under the administration of George Washington." In his March 4, 1861 Inaugural Address, Lincoln stated, "I have no purpose, directly or indirectly, to interfere with the institution of slavery in states where it exists." Even in his famous Emancipation Proclamation, Lincoln promised safety for slavery if Southerners would rejoin the Union. The Proclamation did not free slaves that were living under the flag of the United States, even in the occupied South, but declared free the slaves living in the Confederate States of America. As many Europeans noted, Lincoln pronounced freedom to slaves he could not touch (those in the C.S.A.) and left enslaved those at his very doorsteps (those within the U.S.A.).

Two weeks after this piece of ignorance was inflected upon my ears, Brian Kilmeade, co-host of *Fox and Friends Morning Show*, picked up the anti-South theme. While discussing his book on Sam Houston and the Alamo, Kilmeade stated that "Lincoln offered Houston 50,000 troops to be used to keep Texas in the Union." Kilmeade noted that Houston died before he could see the Union reunited but "at last the Union was saved and everything got back to normal." These are but two of many such "fake-history" statements being poured out upon our people. Why do you think that the number of Southerners who are eager to proclaim pride in Southern history and heritage is going down every year? Do you think that numerous neo-Marxist, fake-history propaganda attacks have anything to do with this decline? And, the most important question: What are we, the members of the Sons of Confederate Veterans, doing to counter this avalanche of fake history?

With Mr. Kilmeade's fake history pronouncements in mind, let us consider the ramification of Lincoln's War upon the Union. Kilmeade noted that Lincoln offered Sam Houston "50,000 troops to *keep* Texas in the Union." The Constitution does not give the president nor congress the authority to appoint a private citizen commander of troops in order to over-rule the will of the people of a state. The obvious question to ask is "How is the Union to be maintained?" According to James Kent, author of *Commentaries On American Law* (1826), the only way the Union can be maintained is "on the concurrence and good will of the parts." Mr. Kilmeade, CONCURRENCE and GOOD WILL excludes bayonets. What type of union have Lincoln and Kilmeade given us? Surely it is not a union of "GOOD WILL" and we know this is true because the South lost more than two-thirds of a million people including both military and civilian as a result of the War. The South was put to the torch, all means of food production and medical supplies were destroyed by the invader making starvation and disease the new norm—surely this was not the result of brotherly love and "GOOD WILL." James Kent of New York (as is Mr. Kilmeade) also noted that "CONCURRENCE" is an essential element in maintaining the Union. Agreement or consistency is how the word "concurrence" is defined. Did the people of Texas and/or the South agree to the invasion of their state and the over-throw of their legally elected government? How about "consistency?" Was Lincoln acting consistently with American history when ordering an invasion of the Southern States? The Declaration of Independence tells us that the people have an unalienable right to "alter or abolish" any government that they no longer desire to be a part of. To alter or abolish a government is the act of a people who live under a government of the "CONSENT of the governed"—a very American principle. Did not the people of Texas secede from Mexico by the free will (consent) of the people? Did not these same people freely join (consent) the Union and did not these same people freely secede (consent) from that Union when it no longer served their needs? It is obvious that the people of Texas and the South were acting with consistency when they, by their consent, "altered or abolished" the Union. Duped Americans, such as Mr. Kilmeade, need to learn the hard lesson that Lincoln did not *save* the Union; Lincoln *transformed* the Union into something America's Founding Fathers had rejected—a supreme indivisible and all-powerful central government. Where once a union created by consent and maintained by the "goodwill and concurrence" of the members stood, a union of coercion created by brute force and bloody bayonets replaced it—exit the American principle of "government by the *consent* of the governed." Yes Mr. Kilmeade, we Southerners are in the Union now but it is not the Union of the Founding Fathers. The Post-Lincoln Union is like unto the "union of a wolf's jaw and the throat of a lamb." Few lambs will "consent" to this form of union, which is why force must be used to ensure that the union will be saved!

According to the worshipers of Lincoln, the trampling upon the Constitution, the invasion and destruction of the Confederate States of America, and nullifying the very soul and meaning of the Declaration of Independence, that is, "the consent of the governed," "the right to alter or abolish any government," and the right to "establish a new government most likely to effect their safety and happiness," was "necessary" in order to save the Union. The cry of "necessity" is the prime tool of all tyrants who are seeking to subvert the rights and freedoms of the people. In *Paradise Lost*, John Milton notes, "So spake the fiend, and with NECESSITY, the tyrant's plea, excused his devilish deeds." Lincoln's "devilish deeds" were and continue to be hidden by the "tyrant's plea" of necessity. But was it necessary? No man embodies the spirit of America's Founding Fathers more so than Patrick Henry. Patrick Henry puts all Americans on notice of true American "NECESSITY" when he stated: "The first thing I have at heart is American *liberty,* the second thing is American *union.*" In a liberty-based society, liberty always trumps government. One cannot be faithful to Patrick Henry's Americanism while embracing Abraham Lincoln's Americanism—one believes in the supremacy of liberty, while the other believes in the supremacy of government. With Lincoln's victory, the

United States became the very thing General Robert E. Lee feared, a nation that is "aggressive abroad and despotic at home."

A noted Founding Father from Virginia, Saint George Tucker, spoke out against all forms of slavery including what he called "political slavery.' He warned that when a government exists not by consent but by force and coercion, the citizens have become slaves of the government. Sixty years later Lysander Spooner, a Radical Abolitionist from Massachusetts, declared that by forcing the South back into a union that they did not desire to be a part of, the United States was increasing slavery not decreasing slavery. Spooner stated, "there is no difference in principle—only in degree—between political slavery and chattel slavery." This truth is obvious, "If you can't leave, you are not free!" But Deep State operatives and other Lincoln lovers embrace political slavery because an all-powerful, indivisible government offers many perks and privileges to those close to the government. This is one reason Fredrick Engels, co-author with Marx of the *Communist Manifesto*, praised Lincoln's effort in promoting "a single and indivisible republic." Tyrannical governments are always proclaiming themselves to be "indivisible."

With your assistance, the SCV can continue its drive to "take back the narrative" and offer our fellow Americans the truth about the War for Southern Independence. Your membership in the Confederate Legion and your camp's support of our various efforts, radio ads, letters to community opinion molders, distribution of *Southern Defenders* and using social media to get the word out about the Sons of Confederate Veteran's defense of Traditional American Values will secure our place in history (we will be making history). Even more important, we will transmit to future generations of Southerners and Americans the good news about our beloved Dixie.

LIBERAL PROPAGANDA AT ITS WORST

The following article was written in 2015 in response to a typical, liberal, anti-South hit-piece published by the Washington Post. It is sad to read such accounts but sadder still is the lack of a bold and robust response by the Southern Rights Movement. This article was written before the establishment of the Southern Victory Campaign by the SCV. It has been the hope of all of those involved in the Sothern Victory Campaign (Confederate Legion, Make Dixie Great Again are vital parts of this campaign) that Southerners will join in the effort to put together an organization that can not only refute neo-Marxist lies but ultimately defeat and destroy our enemies. As has been said so often: "If not us, who? If not now, when?

The lying liberals of the left-wing media never miss a chance to trash Southern heritage. In a recent (08/17/2015) *Washington Post* article chronicling the numerous "Confederate Flag rallies" held since the Charleston church massacre, anti-South bigotry infused every paragraph. As pointed out in chapter 13, 'The Yankee Campaign of Cultural Genocide,' [chapter 17, 3rd edition] in *The South Was Right!*, the South has long been the target of hatred and vilification by "those people" outside the South. This attack upon all things Southern began long before the War for Southern Independence and, as current events prove, continues today.

According to the *Washington Post* article, although many Southerners proclaim that their love for the flag and the South is rooted in love of home and heritage, the root cause of this display is racism, intolerance, and ignorance. Where does the *Washington Post* get their facts about this evil characteristic of Southerners? Their "facts" about Southerners come from the Southern Poverty Law Center (SPLC)! The SPLC is a left-wing hate group that labels anyone to the right of Karl Marx as a racist. According to the SPLC "historians of the South" and "political scientists" who have investigated "the motivations of people who wave the flag, generally dispute this claim." Does anyone believe that an acknowledged and declared enemy of the South (SPLC) will honestly and fairly investigate why Southerners love their heritage? Who are these "historians" and "political scientists"? I am sure Dr. Clyde Wilson, Dr.

Don Livingston, Dr. Marshall DeRosa, or any historian or political scientist with strong pro-Southern views was *not* interviewed.

Even the photograph that led the story about Confederate Flag rallies promoted the idea of a racist, hate-filled South. The photograph that led the story showed two males holding what appeared to be assault rifles and dressed in black "wife beater" undershirts. In another story, the author of an article about the raising of the CSS *Georgia* in Savannah, Georgia, used the article to inform his readers that the Confederates sunk this ship when it could no longer be used to defend the right to own slaves. Thus, the campaign of Southern cultural genocide continues—the left-wing media response to a culture it does not like, just as radical Muslim members of ISIS respond to a culture they don't like.

Unless those of us who love our heritage and rights join together in an effort, such as Radio Free Dixie, to counter this anti-South bigotry, all things Southern will be wiped as clean as Hilary Clinton's hard drive. The time for real pro-active action is now! Let's get Radio Free Dixie going throughout the South.

Chapter XIV

VICTORY: YES, WE CAN!

> We must combine to resist, and that effectually, these encroachments, or the little upon which we now barely subsist will be taken from us.
>
> —John Randolph of Roanoke

WITH EVERY CONFEDERATE MONUMENT under attack and many coming down, it has been difficult to watch or read the news reports lately. Yes, we are living through a cultural crisis. The neo-Marxist agents of destruction seem to have the upper hand. One side gets to tell its side of the story while the Southern view is shunned and ignored by all branches of the media, academia, religious, and political establishments. In the market place of ideas, Southerners find that they must attempt to advance their ideas in a very adversarial market-place. If Southern culture is to survive, we must do as John Randolph of Roanoke suggested and "combine to resist, and that effectually...or the little upon which we now barely subsist will be taken from us." Before we can "combine to resist... effectually," we must consider how we got to this dreadful position.

At the end of the "active" phase of Reconstruction a more or less informal or tacit agreement was reached between the North and South. Southern leaders such as Senator L.Q.C. Lamar of Mississippi signaled this "coming together again" effort when he, a former Confederate officer and Confederate diplomat, gave a well-received eulogy for his former foe Senator Charles Sumner of Massachusetts. This tacit agreement essentially said that the South would never again seek the option of secession and accept Union heroes as

American heroes. In return, the South would be allowed control of their state governments and Southern heroes would also be viewed as American heroes. This tacit agreement allowed for the removal of Federal occupation troops, relieving the Federal government of the expense of policing the conquered South and allowed the South to begin the process of working itself out of Northern imposed impoverishment. By the early twentieth century men of the South filled the ranks of the U. S. military, the National Guards of several Southern States formed the 31st U. S. Army Division, AKA, the Dixie Division, the United States Congress approved the coinage of a United States half dollar commemorating "the valor of the Southern soldier," and the U. S. Post Office printed commemorative stamps depicting Confederate soldiers and leaders. In response the South became the most loyal and patriotic section of the "re-united" nation. In simple language, the South has maintained its part of the tacit agreement.

The recent action of the Federal government's proposal of removing the names of all Confederate heroes from its military bases and the banning of all Confederate flags on said bases, the wanton destruction of Confederate monuments, and the banning of the Southern view about this destruction, prove beyond a doubt that this bargain has been broken. The truism "Silence gives consent" is very applicable as it relates to what the establishment in Washington DC has NOT done. While a few (very few) politicians have condemned the destruction of Confederate monuments, these same politicians parrot the neo-Marxist lie that Confederate heroes "fought for slavery" and were "traitors." This gives every loud, looting, lunatic neo-Marxist all the cover they need to continue their attack upon our Southland. It should be obvious to every Southerner that, indeed, the bargain is broken—not by the South but by the Yankee victor. Daniel Webster correctly noted, "A bargain broken on one side is broken on all sides." The question is no longer "is the bargain broken" but, rather, "what shall we now do?"

If any of our Southern heritage is to remain, we must step up and "combine to resist and that effectually or the *little upon which we now subsist will be taken from us*." Watching the constant attack upon the South in his lifetime, John Randolph noted, "The sun never sets on ambition." Neo-Marxists are very ambitious. Recently a BLM spokesman stated that it was not their desire to stop at pulling down Confederate monuments and changing the names of anything named in honor of the Confederacy, but once the South had been purged of all things related to slavery and treason, the States of the South will be forced to pick new state names so no memory of those "horrible slave days" will be remembered. Our neo-Marxist enemies, following the play book of all totalitarian, all-powerful governments, will not stop until the entirety of the South is dropped into the proverbial "Orwellian memory hole!"

As has been stated time after time, the vast majority of Southerners, 65% to 75%, have a positive view of Southern history and heritage. A nation-wide poll in 2017 demonstrated that 54% of all Americans view Southern heritage in a positive light. So why are we losing? As Ron (my twin brother and co-author of *The South Was Right*) and I have often stated, the Southern heritage movement is a reactionary organization, while our enemy is a revolutionary organization. The enemy attacks our heritage and we respond. Responding is good and surely necessary but a purely "responding" or defensive strategy in sports, war, and politics is a sure prescription for ultimate defeat. We must recognize that our neo-Marxist enemies are revolutionaries. The one constant in all revolutionary groups is their ambition. Remember, the sun never sets on ambition. A revolutionary organization is always looking for a means of advancing its goals, while a reactionary organization responds (reacts) to an attack. It's the old story of them pushing *two* steps forward and we push them back *one* step. They are stopped short of their objective and we celebrate a "victory." Yet, we lose ground with each of our so-called victories.

Another problem with reactionary groups is they look for a quick victory. Reactionary groups have a short view of the struggle, while the revolutionary group has a long view of the struggle. Too often you see this displayed by Southern patriots. We start an effort to defeat our enemy and if it does not provide instance success, we give up on the effort. Gentlemen, if you are sick and the doctor prescribes a bottle of medicine, do you go home take one pill and if you don't get well, you damn the doctor and throw the pills away? Winning this battle is like taking medicine. One pill or even one bottle of pills may not solve the problem. To get well you take the long view and day after day take your medicine. My fellow Southerners, we did not get to this position over-night. It took our enemy 160 years to get to this place! They, being revolutionaries, took the long view and step by step advanced their narrative and now they are at our doorstep. The barbarians are no longer at the gates—they have breached the walls and are coming for us!

Two Governments

One reason we are in this position today is because we live under two governments and both are extremely anti-Confederate in sentiment. One government is the supreme and all-powerful Federal government—which includes all state and local governments! It is sad to remember but since Lincoln's victory, we do not live in a Compound Republic like our forefathers gave us but in a unitary, all-powerful, indivisible, and imperial Federal government. All "lesser" governments must kowtow to their Federal master—more's the pity but it's the truth! But as you will notice, it is not the Federal, State, or local governments that are desecrating and pulling down our monuments. Yes, we often call these people a mob but they are merely the "storm troopers" of the evil, hidden and unseen shadow government. This leftist shadow government does the supreme Federal government's dirty work. The "mob" pulling down monuments could not operate without the cover and influence of this leftist shadow government. The leftist media, academia, religious groups, and politicians are the *enablers* of the mob. They have the ability to destroy any political leader that would dare to oppose the mob's agenda. This is why the mob can act but local police will not intervene—the local political establishment will not allow itself to become the subject of leftist scorn. The leftist shadow government can proceed and do as it pleases but not so for us. If we attempted anything like what the left does, we go straight to jail and no one will pay our bail or lawyers' fees. Let's look at the power of the leftist shadow government.

Who made NFL Saint's quarterback Drew Brees apologize for saying in effect that "all lives matter"? It was not the Federal government but the shadow government that trampled upon his First Amendment Right of Free Speech. I don't follow soccer but I understand that recently a famous soccer player had to go public and denounce his wife for a Twitter comment she made as it relates to Black Lives Matters! Denouncing one's family members is an intimidation technique taken right from the communist playbook! In the past this would have never been condoned. Nevertheless, in politically correct America enforced public criticism of family members has already started. These two incidents demonstrate the power of the leftist shadow government. As John C. Calhoun noted, power can only be resisted by a counter-power. We need **our** own shadow government—a Provisional Government as described in *Dixie Rising: Rules for Rebels* 2nd edition.

Any good military leader understands that you never give the enemy the battle he wants to fight. Reactionaries, those who stay on the defensive, usually will engage the enemy on the battlefield the enemy desires to fight upon—this is a prime example of "fighting dumb!" If we want to win, we must start fighting "smart."

The latest polling information on how the Southern public feels about Confederate monuments and flags demonstrates that from 65% to 75% of Southerners have positive feelings about Southern heritage. Yesterday I read that a *Fox News* poll showed that **only 32%** of Americans agreed with the destruction of Confederate monuments—this is our strength and our enemies' weakness. This is why they want us to meet them in the streets and "fight it out." The pro-South Southern support would evaporate if we were viewed as being as reprehensible as the neo-Marxists rioting in the streets. But if something positive is not done soon, that support will be lost due to the constant barrage of anti-South propaganda being dumped upon our people. Propaganda works, that is why we must provide an alternative view to the neo-Marxist narrative. But we can't rely upon our enemy giving us a fair chance of telling our story. That is why the SCV has created tools, or if you prefer, weapons, to "take back the narrative."

The tools created and provided to our members by the Confederate Legion do little good if we don't use them and if that effort does not have an endpoint. If embraced and used by our membership, these tools can become the foundation for our pressure group, that is, *our* shadow (provisional) government. Remember, 70% of Southerners agree with us. We do not have to have the same size of "propaganda" apparatus as the left—we have the home field advantage! Politicians yield to the pressure of the radical socialists even though 70% of Southerners do not agree with the left's view of the South. Why? Because as Calhoun noted, the only way to resist a tendency is with a counter tendency. By increasing the social footprint of the SCV in the local community and by "educate to motivate, to activate" that Southern 70% to become loud, that is, calling their elected officials, calling into talk radio to defend the South, writing letters to the editor, and VOTING to punish scalawags and elect Southern patriots, we can WIN! Establishing our shadow government is fully covered in the little booklet, *Dixie Rising: Rules for Rebels*. Yes, this is something different from what we have done before but, gentlemen, we cannot keep doing the same ole thing and expect to win this battle. Cleaning cemeteries is good, cleaning tombstones is laudable and raising giant flags is admirable but if we don't win the hearts and minds of our people (convert passive supporters into active supporters) your cemeteries and tombstones will be destroyed. What that giant flag means to you is not the message younger generations of Southerners are being taught. A flag or a monument cannot speak. Those things can only evoke the feelings someone has placed within the "heart and mind" of an individual. Positive pro-South feelings will be placed into the next generation by our use of these Confederate Legion tools or the next generation will absorb the neo-Marxist narrative!

In summary just let me say, the bargain is broken! The table is now reset, all options are available to us. It's time to make them respond to us. We must take the long view, we must fight smart, we must not give the enemy the battle he wants to fight, and we as SCV members and as Americans must stop being reactionaries. We must find a way to have one of OUR people, who has a proven record of fighting for Southern Rights, elected to an office high enough to become the speaker for us on the political stage. In other words, we need someone in a "Bully-Pulpit" to command the attention of our people and the leftist political establishment. Yes, I understand that the SCV is "non-political" but as private citizens we can support and work for men who share our vision of the Southland. Again, read about this in *Dixie Rising: Rules for Rebels*.

Yes, we are in a crisis but we are also presented with a grand opportunity to shake up the present establishment like it has not been since 1861. Make them respond to us, never take anything off the table, make them wonder and worry about, "What the hell are those Southerners going to do next." Put the sker on 'em and keep the sker on 'em. What worked for Forrest will work for us.

LAST OF THE GOOD OLE DAYS

The following article points out the necessity of being victorious in our efforts of regaining a free country for our children. Yes, as this article notes, the author did live in the "last of the good ole days." But it also points out that we can retake the high-ground of free government and bequeath to future generations of Southerners a new and improved "good ole days" for them and their children. Deo Vindice!

Many years ago, as a young father while working with my son, we stopped and talked about what life was like when I was young. We especially talked about how people back then took care of each other and did not depend upon government. The close family/community relationship that I took for granted back then intrigued him. After thinking about what had been said, he made the comment that "You lived in the last of the good ole days." That was over thirty-five years ago and at that time I did not agree with him, but as time goes on, I am more inclined to agree with my son's evaluation of the community standards of today.

In *Plain Folk of the Old South,* Frank L. Owsley notes the extremely close relationship that existed among the Plain Folks in the antebellum South. The Plain Folks did not depend upon government for their well-being but rather snubbed the thought of governmental interference. This tendency of working and depending on each other was noted in the way the Plain Folk of the South would plan their "protracted meetings." Now if you were a member of the "last of the good ole days" crowd, you would understand that this is what is now misnamed by the modern protestant church as a "revival meeting." The Plain Folks of the antebellum South would, after their crops were "laid by," gather at their churches to hold a protracted meeting. The meeting would last until God sent revival to his people. As members of the Pearl Valley, Mississippi community, Ron and I remember working through June and July to get the crops laid by, usually by the third week in July, so we could get ready for our protracted meeting! Yes, we did live in the last of the good ole days.

Having lived during those great days and being instructed by those with firsthand knowledge of the Old South, gleaned from many Confederate Veterans, the Kennedy Twins often wondered how we could pass on the story of the real South to the present and future generations of Southerners. Uncle Seth has the answer. By telling short, interesting stories, Uncle Seth tries to pass on the real story of the South. This is why *Uncle Seth Fought the Yankees* was written; hopefully Uncle Seth will be successful in educating a new generation of Southerners. By educating Southerners, we may yet be able to take back that which has been lost and establish for future generations of Southerners a civil and free society—a society where government exists for the benefit of the people and not one where the people exist for the benefit of the Deep State government. Let us shoulder the burden of retaking the high-ground of free government. We can do this!

Chapter XV

THE STAB IN THE BACK

IT HAS OFTEN BEEN SAID THAT, "A pretended friend is worse than an avowed enemy." The actions of the feeble and submissive "conservative" members of the Mississippi legislature as they abandoned the REAL Mississippi flag, is a recent example of the veracity of that statement. Mississippi's example, along with South Carolina's political whore, Nikki Haley's example, is proof positive that we, as Southern Rights advocates, must do much more to advance our pro-South narrative.

Think of what would happen when feeble and submissive "conservative leaders" recognize that we, members of the SCV, are now a powerful force for Southern Rights. Think of the positive results for our Cause when weak, feeble, and submissive politicians recognize that they must deal faithfully with us **or** face a loud public outcry that will resonate at the ballot box! They may not like us but if they fear what we can do because of our influence, they will hesitate to "stab us in the back" as they have done so often in the past. As John C. Calhoun noted, "Power can only be resisted by power and tendency by tendency." We must be that counter-power and tendency or else we will continue to get more Nikki Haley-type-of results!

There is an obvious question to be asked: How does the SCV offer a counter-power and tendency? This can only be done if the SCV, from top leadership to the newest camp member, dedicates itself to engaging our neo-Marxist enemies in a battle they are not prepared to fight. Here is how you and your camp can strike back at our enemies. Every two months during the year (unless prevented by a pandemic or a natural disaster), the Confederate Legion sponsors a Confederate Counter-Attack. For example, during November and December we will attack FALSE HISTORY by informing the public about the REAL first Thanksgiving and Christmas in Dixie. Several sixty-second radio ads will be produced and the Confederate Legion will purchase air time on many radio stations promoting this effort. These ads will point the general public to our Make Dixie Great Again website where videos and articles are available which point out how the South has become the subject of FALSE HISTORY. This false history is used by neo-Marxists to support their effort of Southern cultural genocide. These ads will also inform the public how to contact the SCV and why they should be proud of our Southern heritage.

What the national SCV, via the Confederate Legion, is doing in selected radio markets, local camps can also do in their market area. Every SCV Camp is encouraged to download these radio ads (found on Make Dixie Great Again website) and purchase air time in their local market area. We will also post sample letters SCV Camps can download and send to local social groups and political leaders. Remember, many of these people will not even know who and what the SCV is all about. It is by communicating with civic, social, religious and political groups that we will increase the general public's knowledge about us. We are creating and publishing pamphlets and handouts such as the 'Southern Defender' to help get our message and name out. The 'Southern Defender' can be inserted in the local newspaper, given out at gun shows, living history events, or just simply left in every waiting room in your area. A BIG plus that is generated by these efforts is that the political establishment—such as the spineless "feeble and submissive" representatives in the Mississippi legislature—will be put on notice that we are building a large fighting force to defend and promote our Rights. Until these feeble and submissive politicians fear what we can do to them, they will continue to be unfaithful friends or more correctly just simple "pretended friends." These pretended friends love us for our votes but don't want to be seen or associated with us—that must and will change!

Every two months the Confederate Legion sends out e-mail alerts to SCV camps asking each camp to become an activist camp in this effort. If every SCV camp would do so, within the next two or three years, the name of the SCV would become a recognized force, respected by and loved by the 70 percent of Southerners who already agree with us, and, most importantly, feared by the pretended friends of the South. We can make a difference but only if we become activists in the Cause of the South. Although celebrating our ancestor's courage and dedication is honorable, being courageous and dedicated to vindicating the Cause for which they fought is what we are called to do—remember General S. D. Lee's charge to us. You can make a difference by joining the Confederate Legion and insisting that your camp participates in these Confederate Counter-Attacks. At the next meeting of your camp, inquire of the camp leadership if they are getting a current e-mail alert from the Confederate Legion. Make the membership aware about what is going on with these counter-attacks and ask about what your camp needs to be doing this month to promote the current counter-attack.

As we have insisted from day one of this "take back the narrative" effort, it is more than Confederate monuments and Southern history that is under attack. A full blown "cancel culture" effort is underway in modern America. The first culture that has been targeted by these left-wing cancel culture loons is of course Southern Culture. The cancel culture movement goes by many names: cultural cleansing, cultural genocide, or just political correctness. Regardless of what we call this plague on the right of free expression and speech, it is totally anti-American. Traditional values as embraced by those who hold dear a Biblical world view and strict-construction Constitutionalism are anathema to left-wing looters and other progressives. Those attacking Traditional American Values from the Ten Commandments to Confederate monuments may call themselves "progressives" but at bottom they are neo-Marxists. Their ultimate goal is the destruction of Western Civilization along with Traditional American Values including our freedom and liberty. Americans must be taught that if the neo-Marxists can have a Confederate monument or flag removed because it "offends" someone, the same thing will happen to the display of a Christmas nativity scene, a Christian flag, or the display of the Ten Commandments when these items "offend" the right person.

The South's firm stand for States' Rights is the one great reason that neo-Marxist continue their attack upon all things Southern. This is not something new. In 1894 Robert Ingersoll, a secular humanist free-thinker and former officer in the Union Army—the army that denied the people of the South the right to live under a government by the consent of the governed—had this to say about

States' Rights: "The great stumbling block, the great obstacle in Lincoln's way and in the way of thousands, was the old doctrine of State's Rights." Yes, the South's adherence to real States' Rights has long been a stumbling block in the way of those people who love an all-powerful big government, AKA, tyranny. Lincoln's victory over "we the people" of the Confederate States of American did not just make all-powerful, big government possible, it made it a reality. This reality is being dealt with each day not just by Southerners but by all Americans. No wonder General Robert E. Lee bemoaned the loss of REAL States' Rights as the harbinger of an "aggressive abroad and despotic at home" United States of America. This being true, it only gives us more reason to redouble our efforts in the SCV to get our message out to our fellow American in general and to our fellow Southerners in particular. Liberty does not defend itself; we must do the work necessary to protect our Rights and secure the Rights and Liberty of future generations of Americans and Southerners.

Rebels in the Republican Ranks

The following article was written in 2005 and in many ways warned that the G.O.P. had already planned to stab the South in the back. Note that this article was written BEFORE Nicki Haley's treachery or the Mississippi RINOs in the State legislature snubbed the democratic will of the people of Mississippi by abandoning Mississippi's traditional State flag for the ugliest flag in the Union. As this article notes, it is time for considering some radical alternatives to passive submission to neo-Marxist tyranny.

Southern conservatives awoke the 15th of July, 2005, to read the following headline in many local papers: "G.O.P. Apologies to NAACP for Southern Strategy." For many Southerners this was somewhat of a rude awaking that hot, Southern July morning. Once again, Southerners are instructed to assume their assigned position upon the "stool of everlasting repentance." As America's formal whipping boy, the South is once again brought into the public eye and given its 30 lashes-this time by our good friends in the National Republican Party. The irony of those words "G.O.P. Apologies to NAACP for Southern Strategy" has not been overlooked by many neo-Confederates. The South, the region that has made the G.O.P. a majority party, must once again stand before the nation, hat in hand, and accept being held up before the world and proclaimed to be the bastion of all that is evil in America. Southerners routinely vote overwhelmingly for conservative candidates; yet, it is the South that is chastised by the G.O.P. in order to curry favor from a group that routinely votes 95% AGAINST conservative candidates. Today, more than anyone in the United States, we the people of the South have made the Republican Party the majority party in America. Yet how is the Republican Party repaying the South?

Let us face the issue squarely; the South is a pariah, a black sheep, the redheaded stepchild, or more correctly, the bastard spurious issue of the Republican Party. Ironic, yes, but the closely held attitude about the South by the National Republican Party does not come as a surprise to those who have been active in the defense of Southern Rights and true American Constitutional government. Southerners instinctively understand that left of center, big government, and socialist elements in America naturally dislike the South. Why would they not hate the

South? After all, the South is the section of America that has from the beginning of the republic stood in the way of the growth of big government. Big governments, whether in the form of Hitler's Nazis, Stalin's communists or America's left-of-center politicians, all place their ultimate faith in government as the agent of change within a nation. Add to this list of big government advocates, America's neo-conservative (neo-con) establishment.

Although dubbed "right of center," America's neo-conservatives, i.e., conservative Republican ideologues, AKA, RINOs, have one thing in common with their socialist allies—their willingness to use the power of big government to advance their policies and/or power. To a neo-con big government is only evil if it is in the hands of their political enemies. As long as conservatives, i.e., neo-cons, are holding the reins of power, big government is not so bad, or so their logic goes. A prime example of this neocon philosophy at work can be seen in the writings of Mr. Neo-Con himself, Newt Gingrich. In his book *To Renew America* (which should have been sub-titled By Trashing the South), Gingrich opens his tome with a blistering attack on Southern racism.

A foundational premise of most neo-cons such as Gingrich is that the South is responsible for all of America's race problems because it is the South who enslaved Blacks, segregated Blacks and of course lynched and otherwise mistreated Black Americans. The left-of-center elements in America routinely assert that Southerners left no stone unturned to "keep the Blackman poverty ridden, ignorant, and otherwise abused." By not stating their opposition to these lies, neo-cons such as Mr. Gingrich have given their tacit approval of this liberal message. In his book Mr. Gingrich states that Southern Democrats established segregation. This "blame the South" mentality is rather common in the left-of-center socialist (liberal) brigades and their neo-conservative comrades. But as is so often the case when dealing with facts about issues of race in America, the truth is stranger than accepted myths. Let's enlighten our neo-con friends with a little history lesson.

Segregation did not begin in the South but rather it began in New England! Also, it should be noted that it was not Southern Democrats who made segregation the law of the land but rather, it was the Federal Supreme Court. In its 1898 *Plessy v. Ferguson* decision the

United States Supreme Court codified racial segregation laws (the so-called Jim Crow laws) as the law of the land. This decision was based upon an 1845 law in Massachusetts (not Mississippi) that mandated separate schools for White and Black children in that good ole Yankee State. The Federal Supreme Court Judge who wrote the majority opinion for this case was a native of the Yankee State of Michigan (not Mississippi). The only judge who voted against the majority of Federal Supreme Court Judges establishing Jim Crow laws in the United States was a Southerner, the only Southerner on the Supreme Court at that time.

Oh look, another bit of irony! Massachusetts and the Federal Supreme Court are responsible for legalizing segregation in the United States. The only Federal Judge to vote against legalizing segregation in the United States was from the South, while those voting for segregation were from the North. Yet, according to the left-of-center neocon crowd, which of course includes Mr. Gingrich, the South is at fault for establishing segregation in America. *Yankees find it very convenient having the South around to blame for all race related problems that face our nation.* Yankees have been given a pass on their history of race discrimination while they waste no time in pointing out the problems down South. Those accustomed to denigrating the South seldom mention the positive contributions made by black and white Southerners. During the days of segregation when few African Americans exercised the right of voting, more schools and colleges were created and funded by white voters of the South than *any nation on earth*. Nowhere in the world, outside of the United States, have black people achieved a higher income, more personal wealth, higher literacy rate, a longer life expectancy or lower infant mortality rate than in the South. While denigrating the South, Mr. Gingrich could find no place in his book to praise the South for its positive contributions to African-Americans. Contrast the difference between the words of the G.O.P. apologizing to the NAACP for their so-called Southern strategy to the words of Booker T. Washington praising the South for its efforts in assisting African Americans.

In his book, *Up From Slavery* Washington describes how while visiting President McKinley in Atlanta, Georgia, a white man and former slave-holder was asked by the President if he thought it would be wise for the President to visit the Negro school at Tuskegee. Booker

T. Washington states the ex-slaveholder answered the President and said it was the proper thing to do. This and many other such acts of kindness between black and white Southerners are detailed in Washington's book, more proof of positive acts of kindness and good will existing between the races in the South. Unfortunately, these acts are seldom reported. In October of 1957, the Shreveport Times printed an editorial written by the Bureau of Public Relations at Grambling College, a Black College in Grambling, Louisiana. In this editorial the Black author explains how at a recent football game a very large crowd of Black people were present. The crowd was well dressed, drove fine cars, and deported themselves with grace. All of this while many outside the South were reporting only negatively on life in the South for Black people. The editorial states: "No one who looked at the thousands of Negroes...would say that the Southern Negro was held in bondage, a mishandled, unkempt, poverty-stricken, and ignorant lot... . It is unfortunate that this side of Negro life in... the South generally goes unnoticed by the northern press, agitators, political rabble-rousers, and others who would put the good people, white and Negro, in a bad light." Both liberal Democrats and neo-conservative (RINO) Republicans delight in putting the "white and Negro [in the South] in a bad light."

Liberals and neo-cons delight in demeaning the South for its social standards during the days when segregation was the law of the land. According to them, the African American led a precarious life before the victory of the civil rights movement in the late 60s. Yet, when we look at the life of African Americans in 1950 as compared to 2005, we find some remarkable differences. In 1950 70% of African American children were born in two-parent homes, today less than 30% are born in two-parent homes; in 1950 sexually transmitted disease (S.T.D.'s) were infrequently seen in teenage African Americans, today S.T.D.'s are epidemic within this group; today Black on Black murder is so common that if it is reported at all it will be on the back pages of the newspaper. In the past ten years in the United States (some forty years after the civil rights victory) more Black people died at the hands of fellow Blacks than where lynched in the South in the past 150 years! This is not intended to be a defense of segregation or lynching but rather it is an attempt to show the hypocrisy of the far left and RINOs as they deal with the issue of race and the South.

Yes, anti-liberty laws (Jim Crow laws) were common in America for far too long. But Southerners did not force these laws upon the United States. In 1950 New York City was just as segregated as Montgomery, Alabama. At a time when only 48 States were in the Union, Jim Crow laws were part of the legal codes of 26 States. Yet it is the South that is blamed for so-called Jim Crow laws.

One hundred and twenty years before the birth of Martin Luther King, Jr. and 176 years before the modern civil rights movement, a founding father of this nation and a Southerner, St. George Tucker of Virginia, wrote an article declaring the need to end both slavery and laws that discriminated against people of color. Oh, yet another irony! While Massachusetts holds the dubious honor of being the first American colony that was engaged in the African slave-trade and the first American colony that passed a law recognizing a master's right in the property of his slaves; it was the South that first demanded an end to the African slave-trade and a Southerner who first demanded equal rights for African Americans. But what about the neocon's (AKA, Republicans) assertion that only the Federal government can protect the rights of a minority?

What a slap in the face neocons give African Americans when they assert that only the Federal government can guarantee the rights of African Americans. Every minority group in American has had to overcome discrimination and each has done so without the guiding hand of big government. Long before signs stating, "No Negroes need apply," signs read, "No Irish need apply." A complete list of such people "discriminated" against in America would include almost the entire American population. Red, Yellow, Black and White, all in their turn have had to face down discrimination. Other than African Americans, no group of Americans has had to have the Federal government "guarantee" their rights. The question then is, "How do people overcome discrimination?" Here is how Booker T. Washington suggested this be done, "The great human law that in the end recognizes and rewards merit is everlasting and universal.... No race that has anything to contribute to the markets of the world is long in any degree ostracized." Hard work and merit, not un-Constitutional Federal rules, edicts and regulations were Booker T. Washington's suggestion for ending discrimination.

It was merit and not Federal bayonets that broke down the color barrier in baseball. Motown was the capital of Black music in the early 1960s, yet Southern white children were just as likely to listen, sing, and buy Motown music as any Northern child. It was merit not Federal bayonets that broke down that color barrier. When Black musician Charlie Pride burst upon the Country Music charts, it was merit and not Federal bayonets that broke the color barrier. The growing economic power of America's African America community, coupled with hard work and merit, would have done a much better job of ending Jim Crow laws in America than empowering the Federal government with fraudulent powers—powers that would eventually be used to speed the growth of big government. As long as the civil rights movement followed Booker T. Washington's model of self-improvement and merit, real progress was possible. This was done without creating an oppressive, big-government overlord interfering with the daily activity of Americans.

Since the rise of the modern civil rights movement, Booker T. Washington's plan of self-improvement has been abandoned and replaced by W.E.B. DuBois' Marxist theory of class struggle. DuBois, an admirer of communism, redefined the civil rights struggle to embrace the concept of struggle between the oppressed and the oppressors. Now, white people are no longer seen as Booker T. Washington describes them, i.e., partners in the improvement of Black Americans but now they are redefined as the oppressor. Listen to the language of Al Sharpton or Jesse Jackson [we must now add BLM and Antifa] and you will hear this communist mantra with each speech. How different it would have been for all Americans if this nation had followed the advice of St. George Tucker and Booker T. Washington. States' Rights would have been saved and big government would have died on the vine. But the left-of-center politicians desired the death of States' Rights.

In his book Mr. Gingrich even explains why he sometimes favors big government. According to Gingrich only the Federal government could protect the rights of minorities, therefore, it is only logical that the Federal government exercise the power necessary to protect minorities. Of course, my first question for big-government neo-cons is, "If the Federal government is the sole guardian of our rights, then who shall guard the guards?" According to Thomas Jefferson and James Madison in their famous Kentucky and Virginia Resolves of 1798, it is the people at the local governmental level, i.e., the States, who retain the final say on how they are to be governed. Furthermore, according to these gentlemen the Federal government can only legally exercise the power it has been granted. Any exercise of power that has not been granted to the Federal government via the Constitution is a usurpation of the reserved rights of the people of the States and therefore not Constitutional.

Even high federalists such as Alexander Hamilton noted that in cases where the Federal government went beyond its delegated rights its action would be non-binding upon the States of the Union. Mr. Gingrich and his neo-con cohorts all pay lip service to the concept of States' Rights. But how can States' Rights exist if the Federal government is allowed to usurp any of the reserved rights of the people of the States? What Mr. Gingrich and his neo-con fellow travelers call States' Rights is at best an effeminate shadow of real States' Rights and at worst, nothing more than States' privileges. A State privilege is a right that the Federal government has determined that the people at the local level could at present exercise. In other words, big government is the one who determines every issue, not the people at the local level. What socialist would find anything wrong with this formula? Hitler did not like the concept of local control (States' Rights), he believed in big government; Stalin did not like people at the local level governing themselves (States' Rights), he wanted to rule from Moscow; likewise, Lincoln, American socialists, and neo-cons don't like State's Rights; they want to be in control of the government.

It is clear that left-of-center groups as well as neo-cons do not like real States' Rights. Southerners and other traditional conservatives view States' Rights as the indispensable safeguard for American liberty. What is it about States' Rights that is so important to the maintenance of true American liberty? The grant of power from the States to the Federal government in the Constitution is well defined and specific. Any power, authority, or right which is not delegated to the Federal government or denied to the States is retained by the people of the sovereign States. According to Mr. Jefferson and Mr. Madison, one of those rights is the right and duty of the States to judge for themselves if the Federal government is overstepping its authority.

Looking at the theory that the Federal government will be the guardian of our rights, the question was asked earlier "who shall guard the guards?" The author of the Declaration of Independence (Jefferson) and the father of the Constitution (Madison) give us a clear and unequivocal answer—we the people of the States. States' Rights is the great check upon the Federal government to ensure that it does not overstep its delegated authority thereby becoming a tyrannical government. The right to judge the Constitutionality of an act of the Federal government has not been denied to the States nor has it been delegated solely to the Federal government; therefore, it belongs to the people of the States. Likewise, the right of nullification and/or secession has not been denied to the States nor have they been delegated to the Federal government; therefore, these rights belong to the people of the States.

Real States' Rights is the only way to check the uncontrolled growth of the Federal government. If real States' Rights as just described were active today, does anyone believe that the Federal government would have a 17 trillion-dollar debt [it is now nearing 30 trillion] or control every act or action of citizens in every State? Everything from how much water goes down your toilet to how much money the IRS will allow you to keep comes under the control of the gargantuan Federal government. Neo conservatives who dutifully pay lip service to the concept of States' Rights while denying the right of nullification and/or secession have successfully castrated real States' Rights.

Without real States' Rights the Federal government continues to grow—when will it end? It will not end until the chains that are now being forged are placed securely upon us! Yes, the growth of big government has been slowed from time to time. Nevertheless, even under the leadership of Ronald Regan [ditto for Donald Trump] the size and power of big government continued to grow—why? Why, even when the Congress and the office of the President are in Republican hands, and a majority of Supreme Court justices are Republican appointees, does this malignant growth of big government continue?

The reason for the malignant growth of big government is because the natural check upon the growth of the Federal government was surrendered at Appomattox—don't hold your breath waiting for Rush Limbaugh [this was written before the sad and untimely death of Mr. Limbaugh], Sean Hannity, Newt Gingrich or any neocon to tell America the truth about Appomattox. Is the present Republican Party serving the needs of those who love true American liberty? If we define true American liberty as Jefferson and Madison did in the Kentucky and Virginia Resolves then it is obvious that the present National Republican Party is not the party of liberty but the party of big government. Yes, it is surely a lesser version of a big government party than the Democratic Party but at bottom, it still believes that Washington rules. This was Lincoln's view and it continues today in both major political parties.

When Washington rules, the republic of republics as established by our forefathers is dead. Our dearest interests and rights are held in the hands of those we cannot control, rather, they control us. What would Patrick Henry think of such a government? When Republican National Committee Chairman Ken Mehlman apologized to the NAACP, he stated he was proud to be part of the party of "Lincoln, Harriet Tubman, Sojourner Truth and Fredrick Douglas." He went on to state that he looked forward to "rebuilding the historic relationship between the NAACP and the Republican Party." If this is the kind of party National Republicans are planning, where does that leave the South?

Lincoln and Fredrick Douglas were advocates of big-government activism, not limited government. Where is this activism headed? [The 2020 Summer of Rage with its BLM and ATIFA violence begins to answer that question, asked back in 2005.] Will this activism lead down the road of civil rights for gays, pedophiles, and practitioners of bestiality? Once the brakes have been removed from government there is no telling how far and how fast it will go. The G.O.P. and its neocon RINOs have no more use for the brakes of REAL States' Rights than their liberal cousins. It is time for traditional Southern conservatives to reconsider our options—perhaps both within the G.O.P. and within the Union. When the scorpion's sting is probing us to the quick, it's time to consider some radical alternatives. Deo Vindice!

Chapter XVI

WHERE DO WE GO FROM HERE?

BY THE TIME YOU ARE READING THIS article the current election season, hopefully, will be over. The big question for Southern Patriots is, "Where do we go from here?" How shall we meet the challenge of this "new reality" and is it really new?

Observers of America's political scene have become accustomed to hearing derogatory comments made about Americans who, like most Southern patriots, hold and express traditional American values. Terms such as "bitter clingers," "irredeemable deplorables," "chumps," and lately, "lizard brains," have been hurled against people holding traditional American values. For Southern patriots these spurious charges are all too familiar. After all, we and our Confederate ancestors are routinely besmirched by false charges of "traitors," "defenders of slavery," and of course, "racists." These charges against Southerners and other Americans holding traditional American values have three things in common: (1) The charge is announced with little or no proof to substantiate the charge, (2) the targeted victim is allowed little or no defense against the bogus allegation, and (3) Traditional American Values patriots and Southern patriots are being attacked by the same evil cabal of neo-Marxists.

Two questions were stated in the opening of this article, "How shall we meet this new reality" and "is it really new"? The second part of that question needs to be explored first if Southern heritage/history warriors are to correctly and therefore effectively defend and promote our Rights. No, this attack is not something new! Well before the War, radical abolitionist propaganda was teaching Northerners to hate not only slavery or even slaveholders down South but to hate the South itself. Radical Abolitionist, William Lloyd Garrison, bluntly damned

Southerners (not just slaveholders) as "thieves and adulterers... ruffians who insult, pollute and lacerate helpless women and conspirators against the lives and liberties of New England citizens." Ralph Waldo Emerson's distain for Southerners is displayed in his statement that in the South, "man is an animal, given to pleasure, frivolous, irritable, spending his days in hunting and practicing with deadly weapons... . Such people live for the moment, they have properly no future." These and thousands of other such derogatory anti-South statements reduced the original Union of "mutual respect and goodwill" into a volatile adversarial relationship. It was not just Southerners who recognized this malignant growth of "hate the South" Northern propaganda. On the floor of the United States Congress, Ohio Representative Clement L. Vallandigham excoriated Republicans and fellow Northern Democrats by pointing out that for twenty years (one generation) Northerners had been "taught to hate slavery AND the South." Vallandigham also pointed out that Northerners had been taught not to just hate the South "but to despise" the South.

Even after the defeat of the South, hatred of the South and racial hate was being used to promote Radical Republican power in Washington. In his letter resigning from the Republican Party, Mississippi Senator Hiram Revels, the first African-American United States Senator, noted the use of hate to protect and advance Republican political fortunes in Washington: "The bitterness and hate created...would have long since been obliterated...were it not for some unprincipled men who would keep alive the bitterness of the past and inculcate a hatred between the races, in order that they may aggrandize themselves by office, and its emoluments, to control my people, the effect of which is to degrade them." Today's leftist use of hate by groups such as Antifa or BLM is common practice. From the other side we also see the use of anti-South sectional bigotry for political advantage. When Nikki Haley of South Carolina jumped on the NAACP's anti-Confederate band wagon, it appears that she was doing so to advance her political fortunes within the National Republican Party. When "conservative" legislators of Mississippi called a rogue legislative secession to replace the Mississippi State Flag, this too appears to have been done for selfish political advancement. No, what we are living through is not a new reality—same song, different verse!

The South's neo-Marxist enemies continually use fake history to promote their anti-Confederate, anti-South, and ultimately, anti-American narrative. As noted, neo-Marxists (this term includes, but is not limited to, liberals, progressives, socialists and Marxists) falsely proclaim that our Confederate ancestors were (1) traitors, (2) defenders of slavery, and (3) racists. Each of these neo-Marxist allegations are easily refuted. The charge of treason is based upon the idea that to secede from the Union was un-American and illegal. Yet, as most SCV members understand, the United States of America was founded upon the act of secession. The Declaration of Independence announces to the world, "That whenever any Form of Government becomes destructive of these ends [life liberty and the pursuit of happiness], it is the Right of the People to alter or to abolish it, and to institute new Government." This document clearly states that the only LEGITIMATE government is one which is based upon the "consent of the governed." Two of America's early Constitutional scholars, William Rawle of Pennsylvania and St. George Tucker of Virginia had already announced to the world that the Right of Secession was a reserved right of "we the people" of each sovereign state. In 1803, Tucker, a founding father, wounded veteran of the War for American Independence, and legal scholar, in explaining the nature of American government proclaimed the Right of secession as an American Right—no one called him a traitor. When in 1825, William Rawle published his textbook on the United States Constitution and included one complete chapter on the Right of secession—no one called Rawle a traitor. His textbook was used at the United States Military Academy at West Point as a textbook on the Constitution and later as a reference book on the Constitution. Were the people at West Point traitors for using and keeping such a textbook? The answer to this question is simple but it is an answer that the media and academia will not allow Americans and especially Southerners to hear.

Likewise, the false charge that the Confederate States of America was founded for the purpose of defending and promoting slavery can be quickly disproved. It is noteworthy that one man who promoted this "fake news" concept of the Confederacy was none other than Karl Marx. Every time a neo-Marxist or conservative commentator promotes the concept of the South "fighting to keep their slaves," they are repeating "fake news" as announced by Karl Marx. The fact that Southern slaveholders at their own expense freed more slaves than any nation on earth should give anyone reason to question Karl Marx's opinion of the South. When it comes to the issue of racism, neo-Marxist and conservative commentators never mention that America's racist "Jim Crow" laws were not a creation of the Confederate States of America or any Southern State Court—Jim Crow law is a creation of the United States Supreme Court, see *Plessy v. Ferguson*, 1898. In 1898, of the nine justices of the Supreme Court only one justice voted against establishing "lawful" racial discrimination in the United States and that justice was a Southerner—the only Southerner on the court at that time. Being Southern does not make one a racist.

I am sure that few members of the SCV who read this article are surprised by the preceding information about treason, slavery and racism. As noted above, "the media and academia will not allow Americans and especially Southerners to hear" this information. We are faced with a dilemma. We are in possession of REAL history as opposed to neo-Marxists fake history, but the neo-Marxists are in possession of the "normal" or traditional means of communication—media and academia. At present, 60% to 70% of Southerners respect our view of Southern heritage/history. Nationwide, close to 56% of Americans agree with our view of Southern heritage/history. The problem is that without a robust and creditable promotion of a positive view of Southern heritage/history, these numbers will continue to decrease. Once less than 50% of Southerners view our heritage/history in a positive manner, ALL WILL BE LOST!

When the neo-Marxist view of the South becomes mainstream in Dixie, no one will want to join the SCV. How many people will want to visit an SCV museum when that museum is viewed as an institution promoting treason, racism and hatred? When individuals are fearful of being subjects of neo-Marxist doxing for visiting SCV related events, how many visitors will dare show up at SCV events? This brings us to the question: "Where Do We Go From Here"? One thing is for sure, if we continue doing only those things we are "comfortable" doing or have always done, we will continue to lose support from average Americans and especially Southerners.

It is well past time for SCV camps and members to get out of their comfort zone and take our message to John Q. Public. The Heritage Operations Committee is often asked to buy radio ads in an area where a monument is being removed or our flag is being censored. As money allows, we will respond but the most import ad you run in your community is not the one AFTER an attack takes place but those that run BEFORE said attack takes place. By keeping your community aware of why they should be proud of their Southern heritage and making sure elected officials understand that the Sons of Confederate Veterans are active in their community, we will "nip it in the bud," the "bud" being anti-Confederate attacks. Growing up on a farm, we were often admonished, "After the horse is out, its too late to close the barn door!" Don't wait until you are under attack before you inform your community of the glories of their Southern heritage. Another old truism is applicable also: "An ounce of prevention is worth a pound of cure!" Why is it that members of the Sons of Confederate Veterans cannot seem to understand this truth as it relates to defending and promoting our heritage?

Polishing tombstones, cleaning cemeteries, building state-of-the-art museums, raising giant flags and monuments will not save our heritage—even though this is within our comfort zone. Remember, monuments and flags do not have a voice, we must speak for them. Tombstones and cemeteries cannot speak for themselves; we must speak for them. Unless we get busy telling the REAL story about the men memorialized by these tombstones within those cemeteries, future generations of Southerners will embrace the neo-Marxist fake history narrative. For the past three years the Heritage Operations Committee has been working to provide SCV camps and members with the tools necessary to inform our fellow Southerners about the REAL story of the South and our noble ancestors. You or your camp can buy copies of the Southern Defender and pass them out to members of your community; your camp can download any of our one-minute radio ads and purchase time on your local radio station; you can place our videos from our Make Dixie Great Again website on your social media; and, you can donate to the SCV's Heritage Defense Fund or Confederate Legion which will provide funds to send our message to millions of our fellow citizens.

Let me explain what I just did to assist in this effort. At our SCV website under the tab "Contact" I clicked on the title "Contribute to the Cause" at which time I saw several donation options. You may pick either the "Confederate Legion" or "Heritage Operations Defense Fund" to fund our counter attack against neo-Marxist lies. I selected Heritage Operations Defense Fund and made a $5 monthly donation. If every SCV member would donate $5 per month to either of these funds, we would have almost $150,000.00 monthly to purchase pro-South ad time on radio and T.V. Want to see the SCV on Tucker Carlson's show or any major news program? Then donate and let's get started giving our enemies a real fight! Either we get busy fighting smart or get used to seeing all of our heritage, both Southern and American, cancelled by the leftist mob. The choice is yours—Duty is before us!

DRAINING THE SWAMP

This article was written before the Swamp struck back in November 2020. Always remember, the Constitution is not self-enforcing. Unless we the people of the sovereign states have the power to force the Federal government to abide by the Constitution, Federal tyranny will be the lot of all Americans. Where do we go from here? The answer is in the hearts and hands of this generation of Americans in general and Southerners in particular.

Much has been said lately about "draining the swamp" of big government in Washington, a daunting task to be sure. Although a remarkable metaphor, the task at hand may be more complicated than just digging a ditch and draining off the "waters of corruption."

After the discovery of insects as a vector for the spread of deadly diseases, humans began the process of draining pools of stagnant water to reduce the numbers of disease laden insects. With swamps and other stagnant bodies of water removed, normal healthy living became the norm. Yet sometimes draining the swamp was not possible. If one had built his home on the Okefenokee or Atchafalaya swamps, America's two largest swamps, draining the swamp is an impossible task. When "draining the swamp" has proven to be an impossible task, the only reasonable option is to move (secede) from the noxious infestation. After all, if you can't drain the swamp, it is better to leave than face the scourge of deadly disease.

It would be easier to drain the Okefenokee swamp with a small shovel than put the genie of big government in Washington back into the bottle, i.e., "drain the swamp." It is well beyond the time for rational people to consider better ways of controlling big government, AKA, the "swamp". America's founding fathers understood this necessity when on July 4, 1776, they proclaimed to the world that people had the right to "alter or abolish" any government not to their liking. Moreover, they announced that "we the people" have an unalienable right to form a new government (an act of moving away from the swamp) that met their desire as a free people. Perhaps "we the people" of the occupied Confederate States of America should insist upon the American Right, quoting the Declaration of Independence, to "institute new Government...in such form, as to them shall seem most likely to effect their Safety and Happiness."

Upon issuing that demand, turn to our fellow Americans who love Traditional American Values and say, follow our lead.

The bogus election of 2020 proves that the swamp is indeed too large to drain. Even if a new and improved "conservative" is elected in a subsequent presidential election, the swamp will only retreat a little, allow Americans to calm down, and then reassert its power over we the people. Unless REAL States' Rights, inclusive of the rights of nullification and secession, are recognized, the pestilence of the swamp will be in our children's future.

Chapter XVII

TOWARD THE LIBERATION OF SOUTHERN STATES

ACCORDING TO AN ARTICLE posted on National Review Online, January 13, 2021, Representative Alexandria Ocasio-Cortez (AOC), Dem. NY 14th Congressional District, opined that the South must be "liberated." She continued in her tirade against the South as if all the evils of the world resided deep in the heart of Dixie. For those of us who have been fighting against neo-Marxist lies about our Southland, AOC's disgusting remarks are not shocking. In the January/February 2021 issue of the Confederate Veteran's 'Forward the Colors,' I stated that it has become common place for Americans holding Traditional American Values to hear "derogatory comments...such as 'bitter clingers,' 'irredeemable deplorables,' 'chumps,' and lately, 'lizard brains'" directed toward themselves. So, AOC's remarks are not shocking so much as they are revealing.

Such anti-South bigotry as displayed by AOC is not new in American politics. Anti-South bigotry started to grow as soon as "those people" understood that the South stood in the way of the North's self-aggrandizement. In January 1863, upon the floor of the House of Representatives, Ohio Representative, Clement L. Vallandigham, speaking to his fellow Northerners noted, "You have utterly, signally, disastrously—failed to subdue millions of 'rebels,' whom you had taught the people of the North and West not only to hate but to despise." Notice how Vallandigham insisted that Southerners had been made the object of derision and hate by those who controlled the new all-powerful Federal government.

Less one thinks that this anti-South bigotry was something that arose in response to the South's struggle for independence, consider the words of the Founding Fathers. Patrick Henry warned that the South, composing a minority in the new union, could not prevent the North from using the South as the "milk-cow" of the union. Henry noted, "When oppressions may take place, our representatives may tell us, 'We contended for your interest, but we could not carry our point, because the representatives from Massachusetts, New Hampshire, Connecticut, etc., were against us.' Thus, sir, you may see there is no real responsibility." Henry was pointing out that being a minority, your interests are left in the hands of the majority. Even though we have representatives who are responsible for overseeing our interests, what good is that "responsibility" when one is out voted? Rawlins Lowndes of South Carolina believed that with the union under the control of the North, "the sun of the Southern States would set, never to rise again." Joseph Taylor warned, "We see plainly that men who come from New England are different from us...They cannot with safety legislate for us." These warnings were warnings against becoming the victim of Northern enrichment at the expense of the South. From the North's perspective, the South had to be destroyed if money and wealth was to continue to flow from the pockets of Southerners into the pockets of Northerners.

The first step in the destruction of the South was to demonize all Southerners, not just the minority of Southerners who owned slaves, but all Southerners—this demonizing continues to this day! Howard Floan noted that William Lloyd Garrison's "hatred of slavery became hatred of the slaveholder, and the slaveholder became indistinguishable from the Southerner." Garrison often damned Southerners as "thieves and adulterers...ruffians who pollute and lacerate helpless women and conspirators against the lives and liberties of New England." On the floor of the United States House of Representatives, Republican Representative Joshua Giddings gave voice to his anti-South bigotry when he noted his desire for the time "when the torch of the incendiary shall light up the towns and cities of the South." Yankee bigoty is uniquely displayed by Ralph Waldo Emerson, who suggested that in the South, "man is an animal, given to pleasure, frivolous, irritable, spending his days in hunting and practicing with deadly weapons to defend himself against his slaves and against his companions brought up in the same idle and dangerous way. Such people live for the moment, they have properly no future."

When reading or hearing the current anti-South bias that is spewed in all forms of media and by current elected representatives, one is struck with one overriding fact: Same song, different verse. We have heard it all before. AOC and the neo-Marxist crowd may think that anti-South bigotry is the wave of the future but actually, its "old hat."

Recently while listening to a travel channel program on South Carolina the host, while commenting on the horrors of the Charleston, SC slave market, stated the "40% of all Africans brought to the New World passed through the Charleston slave market." Since Spain introduced slavery into the New World in 1503 and held a virtual monopoly on the African slave trade, it is difficult to believe that Charleston, founded in 1670, could be the "hub" of Western Hemisphere slave trading. Yes, slaves were bought and sold in Charleston but this is not something unique to South Carolina. At the same time, slaves were being bought and sold in New York, Boston, and Philadelphia. The truth is that only 6% of African slaves ever touched the shores of what would become the United States! How can this 6% somehow become "40% of all slaves taken from Africa?" It is easy to spread a lie if no one will ever challenge the liar. In the dark world of ignorance and bigotry, we the members of the Sons of Confederate Veterans are called upon to be "Lighthouses of Truth."

How can we become "Lighthouses of Truth?" Both as private citizens and as SCV Camps, we can do a lot to enlighten the general public about the noble Cause of the South and help restore real Southern pride. As SCV Camps, each camp can take part of our Bi-Monthly "Confederate Counter Attack." Starting in January and every other month thereafter the following Counter Attacks will be pushed: Confederate Diversity, Confederate Veterans/American Veterans, Religion in Dixie, July 4th- America's Secession Holiday, The Constitution and the South, and America's Real Thanksgiving. At our website, www.makedixiegreatagain.com, your camp will find radio ads, videos, articles and letters to community leaders to push our positive narrative about the South. Each SCV camp should start thinking of itself as a local Lighthouse of Truth and use these and other efforts (Dixie Defenders and social media) to answer the darkness of ignorance and anti-South bigotry.

As individuals we should never forget to use our social media accounts to promote a positive image of the South. Take advantage of talk radio call-ins. Sons of Confederate Veterans members should take the time to call in and respond in a positive manner to any challenge to our heritage. One almost forgotten method of getting the word out is a letter-to-the-editor. Usually, a short letter dealing with a topic that is currently in the news has a chance of being published. Don't be disappointed if your letter gets rejected, keep trying with other letters and ask other friends to do the same. I have the most success with weekly papers but occasionally I have had letters published in national journals. Here is an example of a letter that deals not solely with Southern history or politics but it does give the reader a different view about the issue of real States' Rights and secession.

Dear Sir,

The 2020 Presidential election controversy has given rise to many questions about the Electoral College and why Americans elect their President by such a non-democratic system. Most Americans are shocked to learn that if the Electoral College cannot elect a president, the House of Representatives, voting by state with each state having only ONE vote, would determine the president. Many citizens question why Wyoming with only 578,000 population has the same number of votes for president in the House of Representatives as California with almost 40 million population? Yes, this is un-democratic. The justification of this system is embarrassing to conservative and liberal political pundits and shocks many Americans. The embarrassing and shocking answer is that this system of presidential election is done because American States were once sovereign states. State sovereignty is foundational to the idea of secession.

In today's Red State/Blue State divide the idea of peaceful secession has become an appealing approach to deal with America's irreconcilable ideological divide. Many Americans today may recoil at such a suggestion but our sixth president, John Q. Adams of

Massachusetts, advocated secession rather than trying to maintain a union of antagonistic groups. Adams noted, "If the day should ever come... when the affections of the people of the states shall be alienated from each other; when fraternal spirit shall give away to cold indifference... far better it be for the people of the disunited states, to part in friendship from each other, THAN TO BE HELD TOGETHER BY CONSTRAINT."

James Madison insisted that the "safety and happiness" of a society was more important than any government. Madison said that "if the Union was adverse to public happiness, my voice would be...abolish the Union." It is obvious that left-wing Americans and right-wing Americans openly detest each other to the point of near civil war. Why then should we not look to the option of peaceful secession; Red State from Blue State and Red Counties from Blue Counties? This idea may upset the Tucker Carlsons and Rush Limbaughs on the Right but other than continuous animosity and hate, what option is there? It's no longer just Southerners who believe that secession was and still is legal, many Americans are now questioning why people who violently disagree should be forced to remain in the same government. Peaceful secession is the answer. A return to state sovereignty and real States' Rights, which of course includes the right of secession, may yet be in America's future.

Respectfully,

Walter D. Kennedy

Downsville, LA

The main objective of this letter was to get people thinking about why we have an Electoral College. Also, how the Electoral College system relates to the original Constitution which proves that, yes indeed, the South Was Right! Hopefully Americans from all political spectrums will understand that being united at the point of a bloody bayonet is the sure sign of tyranny not freedom.

The irony of making heroes out of men such as John Brown while condemning Osama bin Laden points out just how unfairly the defeated South is still being treated. When radical socialist Alexandria Ocasio-Cortez, U.S. Representative from N.Y., demands the destruction of all things Southern, she is following the lead of men such as John Brown and Osama bin Laden. Until we, the people of the defeated and occupied South, have the ability to check the abuses of the Federal government via REAL States' Rights, these "paradoxes" will continue. The end result of embracing these paradoxes will be the banishing from Ocasio-Cortez's America of all things Southern.

Yankee Paradox

On September 11, 2001, under the direction of Osama bin Laden, Islamic terrorists attacked New York City and Washington, DC. Americans were shocked not only by the violent terrorist attacks but also by the "victory" celebrations held by Islamic radicals around the world. Both the media and average citizens questioned what type of world we lived in when such dastardly acts were not only condoned but celebrated and even greater acts of terror against America were being advocated.

Few Americans today, Northern or Southern, would consider bin Laden and his associates anything other than bloody criminals of the lowest order. Yet, these same people will look upon John Brown as a hero and great defender of the downtrodden. Both men committed acts that were beyond the pale of civilized warfare and both men killed innocent Americans in order to promote an agenda they believed justified their action. Why is it that one man, bin Laden, is viewed as a blood thirsty terrorist while the other man, John Brown, is an American icon? Here we see the great Yankee paradox: Some terrorists are evil, while other terrorists are good! In the fevered mind of the Yankee, as long as an illegal act is being committed by a Yankee-sponsored terrorist against Southerners it is a heroic act, whereas, if such action is being taken against the people of New York or Washington, i.e., Yankees, it is a terrorist act.

Once again it must be pointed out that as a defeated people the rights and interests, such as our history, our economic welfare, or our civil liberties, must take a back seat to what is useful and good for the victors. John Brown had one objective, be that in Kansas or Virginia, kill Southerners. It did not matter if the Southerner was a non-slave holder or a free man of color, John Brown's higher law authorized his attacking and killing Southerners. This is the same "higher law" thought process that Osama bin Laden used to rationalize his attacks upon Americans on 9-11, yet, Yankees cannot see and Southerners are not allowed to point out such fine distinctions. Until Southerners accept the reality of being a citizen of a defeated nation, the Confederate States of America, a continuation of these Yankee paradoxes will be our lasting lot—regardless of who is elected president.

Chapter XVIII

THE HIGH-FLYING FLAG

WE ARE HAPPY TO ANNOUNCE that the Sons of Confederate Veterans has secured for our use a 24 X 40-foot Confederate Flag aerial banner. This banner has been used several times to protest events such as NASCAR's banning of our beloved flag and to inspire our fellow Southerners. As you will notice in the attached photo, the banner informs the public how to contact the Sons of Confederate Veterans. At future SCV events, don't be surprised if you look up and see our giant flag being towed through the sky by the "Confederate Air Force."

I am sure every member of the SCV will be proud to see our banner displayed but the important thing to remember is that the general public will be reminded that the SCV is on the job of protecting and promoting our heritage. One thing that must be remembered is that a flag cannot speak for itself. When you and I look at our flag we see a banner that we respect as the emblem of a just and noble cause. Unfortunately, what we see and what the general public hears about our flag are two different things. Polls taken on how the Confederate Flag and Southern history is viewed demonstrates that Southerners born before 1970 have a high, up to 90% or more, regard and respect for our flag and history. These same polls reveal that Southerners born after 2000 do not have the same regard and respect for our flag and the South. As the older generations of Southerners die, the younger Southerners are more likely to fall in line with the neo-Marxist view of our beloved banner and Southern history.

What is true about the views of the Confederate Flag and Southern history is also true about most Traditional American (therefore, Southern) Values. In his book, *Be Ye Separate: Bible Belt Revival or Marxist Revolution*, Ron Kennedy noted:

In a recent experiment, random students on a major university campus were shown two books, the Holy Bible and the Communist Manifesto, and asked which book was the most dangerous for society? Without hesitation they selected the Holy Bible as more dangerous than Karl Marx's Communist Manifesto! And remember, the current public educational system is using our tax dollars to indoctrinate our children and grandchildren. Is there any wonder that a recent survey of university-educated young people found that a majority stated that rioting is an acceptable method for social change! This willingness to use violence is the mentality of Mao-Zedong's Red Guards in Communist China circa 1966—during which Chinese students caused the death of thousands of innocent civilians and destroyed over 6,000 historic sites and monuments.

The sad reality of today's educational system is that young people are being "educated" away from traditional values held not only by Southerners but by all Americans.

When we say that a flag or monument cannot speak for itself, we are facing the reality of today's educational, social, and political reality. Sure, you and I see our banner as a positive display of patriotism, love of family and freedom because we were raised in an environment that taught respect for these values. For the most part, our children and grandchildren are taught that these flags and monuments—and even the Bible and Constitution, are hold-overs from an evil "white-supremacy" racist society bent upon crushing people that did not look like them. Since a flag cannot speak, a monument of stone cannot define what it is memorializing, or a clean, well-kept cemetery cannot tell the story of those reposed within its graves, who will speak for them? Unless we of the SCV give a voice to our flag, monuments, and sainted dead, only the neo-Marxist voice will be heard and that voice is loud and blatant.

In a recent T.V. debate with several BLM thugs, I was informed that "Mississippi and the South has not even begun to atone for its evil past. Everything associated with the old Confederacy must be erased, even the names of the States that join the Confederacy must be erased!" In the March/April 2021 issue of the *Confederate Veteran's* "Forward the Colors", I noted that New York Representative, Alexandria Ocasio-Cortez (AOC) suggested that the South needed to be "liberated" from its intrinsic racism. Following the lead of such radicals as BLM and AOC, is it any wonder that United States military bases named after Confederate leaders are now being purged from America? The same group that is pushing these acts of cultural genocide are now demanding the removal of any monument on Federal property such as National Parks at Shiloh, Gettysburg, Vicksburg, etc. These radicals insist that America cannot be cleansed of its "intrinsic racism" until all monuments to "white supremacists" and defenders of slavery are eliminated. Yes, I, like you, understand that these symbols are not what the neo-Marxists claim but their narrative is the only one being heard by the general public and reinforced by the educational system, media and social media platforms.

As bad as all of the aforementioned acts of cultural genocide are, worse acts are being planned. Once the National Parks are purged of "racist" monuments, public law will then demand the shielding of the general public from the "emotional trauma" of having to view noxious symbols of "intrinsic racism" such as Confederate Flags and monuments. All such symbols must be on private property only and a barrier must be placed between said noxious symbols so as to protect the general public from being offended by viewing those symbols. Another suggestion offered by these radicals is the exhumation of the remains of all racist traditors from National Parks and property and said remains "disposed of," not re-buried but disposed of!!! Having dealt with and debated these radicals, I can assure you that their hatred and loathing of the South is that intense.

I am sure at this point there are many readers of this article that have already proclaimed to themselves that, "that will NEVER happen," Americans will not tolerate such. The "never" mentality is not something new.

A SILENT SAM IS COMING TO A COMMUNITY NEAR YOU

In 1994 the photo of a decapitated Confederate monument was published in *The South Was Right!* Various Southern "leaders" said the Kennedys were making too much of this "one-of-a-kind" incident and needed to calm down and don't cause problems. Today there are "Silent Sams" all across the South. People who said it would NEVER happen here, were wrong!

In the late 50s and 60s, radical segregationists wore "NEVER" buttons because they said integration would never happen. They were wrong! Never say a radical change can't happen here. As bad as the Silent Sam incident was, far worse is coming if we don't educate, motivate, and activate John Q. Public. PR is not a luxury or side item for the SCV to consider—it's a life-or-death issue!

During the vote to purge United States Military Bases of names related to the Confederate States of America, many Southern "conservative" Senators and Representatives voted with AOC and her neo-Marxist cohorts. It should be obvious to anyone with half a brain that WE ARE LOSING THIS FIGHT! We are losing because our message is not being told to the general public. Our elected officials will always take the path of least resistance and we, the decedents of Confederate Veterans, offer little or no resistance or threat to their political comfort. While our people are daily distressed by neo-Marxist activism, our elected officials remain very comfortable.

It is well past time for those of us who love liberty more than government and love our Southern heritage, to comfort the distressed and distress the comfortable! How do we, the SCV, comfort the distressed? Our people are distressed because they see what is happening and feel that we who should be leading the fight for our Rights are not doing enough. This is why we initiated the Southern Victory Campaign which includes the Confederate Legion and its Southern Counter attacks. When SCV members and John Q. Public hear our ads on the radio, read our newspaper or internet ads, pick up one of our Southern Defender, or see our posts on social media, they will receive "comfort" in knowing that the truth is being told at last. Just as important as that, the political establishment will begin to view us not as a nuisance but as a real threat to their 'comfort.'

There is a big difference between something that is a nuisance and a threat. A fly buzzing around your head is a nuisance, whereas a coiled Rattle Snake is a deadly threat. The SCV is little more than a nuisance to the establishment. But if each SCV Camp will become an activist camp and join in our effort to "take back the narrative," we will be viewed as a threat to the comfort of the elected establishment. Every other month, the Confederate Legion promotes a Confederate Counter Attack. The CL will provide radio ads, Southern Defenders, and letters your camp can send to civic and elected groups promoting a positive view of our Cause. This type of activity in the local community is seen by our fellow Southerners as well as the political establishment. Little by little, we can effect a change in attitude about who we are and increase the potential of making the establishment very uncomfortable.

As has often been said, the struggle we find ourselves in today is not just a Confederate flag problem. Our Rights of assembly, speech, and having pride for our family are part of the neo-Marxist attack upon traditional American values. Our religious values are being assaulted by the same group of neo-Marxists who are attacking our Right to display pride in our history and heritage. We must use every legitimate means at our disposal to let our fellow citizens know that this fight is not just about the Confederacy but about American values. We must "educate, motivate, and activate" our fellow citizens to the dangers before us and them or one day all freedom will be taken from us as is noted in the following poem:

FIRST THEY CAME AFTER CONFEDERATE MONUMENTS

First, they came to deface Confederate monuments

I did not speak out

Because I have no interest in Confederate monuments.

Then they came to destroy
and pull-down Confederate monuments.

I did not speak out

Because I have no interest in Confederate monuments.

Then they came after Kate Smith because
she sang "God Bless America."

I did not speak out

Because I was not interested in Kate Smith's music.
Then they came with mobs to deface religious statutes

I did not speak out

Because it was just an isolated incident that would never happen here.
Then they came to deface and burn my church

And by now, everyone was fearful to speak-out

No one spoke out in defense of my church.

Then they came for me and my family

And there was no one left

To speak out for me and my family.

Freedom is seldom lost all at once but, thanks to people's apathy,
Freedom is gradually eroded and eventually destroyed.

James R. Kennedy

Don't be so foolish as to believe that it will never happen here! Those who drink from the well of mediocracy and complacency, drink to their own family's enslavement and or death. Don't be a wearer of a "Never" button. Become an activist in the defense of traditional American values, which of course includes all things Southern. Let the words of John Randolph of Roanoke warn and inspire us to the struggle we must fight: "we shall keep to the windward side treason—but we must combine to resist, and that effectually, these encroachments, or that little upon which we now barely subsist will be taken from us." John Randolph did not wear a "Never" button!

Charles Rangel, Rush Limbaugh, and the Confederate Flag

Yes, we have a "high-flying" flag but that flag and all that it represents has been the target of Marxists for many years. The sad fact is that not only do leftists hate and abuse our Southern flag and heritage but they are given "cover" and virtual approval by most conservative commentators. The following article demonstrates how both conservatives and radical liberals unite in their attack upon Southern heritage. Moving from informing about said attack, the article challenges Southerners to join in an effort to take back what is rightfully ours as Americans.

On March 20, 2014 Rep. Charles Rangel—Democrat Harlem District NY—speaking of his political opponents stated: "They are mean, racist people. Because in those red states, they're the same slave-holding states. They had the Confederate flag. They became Dixiecrats, they had the Confederate flag. They are now the Tea Party and they still have the Confederate Flag." As I listened to the fuming tirade of this anti-South bigot, I could not help but remember the words of a great Southern writer, Frank Lawrence Owsley, when in 1930 he stated that the North was determined to, "write error across the pages of Southern history which was out of keeping with the Northern legend, and set the rising and unborn generations of Southerners upon stools of everlasting repentance." Today too many Southerners agree with Rangel!

Rangel was wrong on many points:

- A. Most Red States were not Confederate States; therefore, they had no historical connection to the Confederate flag.
- B. He ignores the history of Blue State slavery:
    - a. Massachusetts *Desire* 1637
    - b. First law protecting slavery Mass. 1642
    - c. First Fugitive Slave law was enacted in New England in 1643
    - d. First segregation of Black school children occurred in New England

e. Negro whipper law passed in Massachusetts
   f. Slavery existed in Massachusetts for more than 70 years longer than in Mississippi
   g. Thirteen strips on United States flag represents the thirteen slave-holding colonies
   h. Northern exclusion laws—such as, Illinois in 1862
   i. 1858, Oregon and California Constitutions excluding Blacks in their states.

Even Right-Wing Conservatives feel free to attack the Confederate flag. Just a few days after Rep. Rangel's illogical and bigoted attack on the Confederate flag, Rush Limbaugh [this was written before the untimely death of Mr. Limbaugh] excoriated and condemned Rangel but not for his ignorant attack upon the South's beloved flag. Rather, Limbaugh, never called Rangel to task for his incorrect knowledge about the South thereby adding credence to Rangel's false statements. Limbaugh joined Rangel by promoting a false history of the Republican Party by stating that it was the Republican Party that "fought to free" African-Americans and the Republican Party was the best friend of men of color—and, paraphrasing Limbaugh, it was the Republican Party that fought against the Confederate flag. Limbaugh, and other "conservative" commentators are simply following Karl Marx's theory about the South when they refuse to tell the truth about Southern history. Too many conservative commentators follow in the steps of Karl Marx's view of the Confederate States of American. Here is how "those people" view Southern/Confederate history:

   a. They repeat the same old worn-out theme of the victor, North equals good; South equals bad: This is American history according to the victor of the War and this narrative has been picked up and vociferously promoted by neo-Marxists.
   b. Both conservative Limbaugh and liberal Rangel overlook the same facts of history when talking about the Confederacy. But what about Limbaugh's assertion that the Republican Party was the political party that

was the friend of African Americans: Hiram Revels, Republican from Mississippi, and the first elected Black United States Senator was elected in 1870. Revels resigned from the Republican Party in disgust due to the misuse of Black and White citizens of Mississippi by the Republican Party. In an 1875 letter to President Grant, Revels noted: "Since reconstruction, the masses of my people have been, as it were, *enslaved* in mind by unprincipled adventurers, who, caring nothing for country, were willing to stoop to anything no matter how infamous, to secure power to themselves, and perpetuate it.... . My people have been told by these schemers, when men have been placed on the ticket who were notoriously corrupt and dishonest, that they must vote for them; that the salvation of the party depended upon it. This is only one of the many means these unprincipled demagogues have devised to perpetuate the *intellectual bondage* of my people.... . The bitterness and hate created by the late civil strife has, in my opinion, been obliterated in this state, except perhaps in some localities, and would have long since been entirely obliterated, were it not for some unprincipled men who would *keep alive* the bitterness of the past, and inculcate a hatred between the races, in order that they may aggrandize themselves by office, and its emoluments, to control my people, the effect of which is to degrade them." Revels is talking about Limbaugh's Republican Party! Like Booker T. Washington stated in his book, *Up From Slavery,* it was the men who carried the Confederate flag who proved to be the best friends of the former slaves—something Limbaugh and Rangel refuse to acknowledge.

Why do both the left and the right elements of America's political establishment hold Southern history and heritage in such low regard?

Richard Weaver, noted Southern philosopher and historian, observed that the South took the defeat at Appomattox too seriously and too literally. The South became the defensive South and never took the offensive—it thereby conceded the moral high ground to the victor. She allowed the victor to even name the war: Civil War, War of the Rebellion, War Between the States are all names that allow the North to take the moral high ground. Civil War: A Civil War is one where two groups within a nation fight for control of the government. In 1861 the South sought to be free from the national government controlled by Yankees, it did not seek to control the Federal government of the United States. This term makes it easy for the victor to say the War was over slavery. The War of the Rebellion: Exercising one's Constitutional Right is not an act of rebellion, this term is a false label. Lincoln, the Republican Party, and the North's trampling upon God-given rights is an act of rebellion against the Constitution. War Between the States: This term is not true because it was not two states but two governments at war.

But what was the struggle of 1861-65 about? The victor will parade two main topics as the cause of the war, slavery and treason. The title War for Southern Independence names the reason the war was fought—Independence. As is pointed out in the Declaration of Independence, the right to consent to the form of government we live with and the right to "alter or abolish" an unfavorable government is foundational to American government.

In modern politics, taking and maintaining the moral high ground is absolutely necessary if one is to be victorious. In a mass democracy, how one feels always trumps logic and facts. Example, States' Rights. Southerners often say, "We fought the War for States' Rights." While historically and constitutionally correct, this statement surrenders the moral high ground to the Yankee. The Yankee and Southern scalawag will reply to your States' Rights argument by saying, "So, you believe in the States' Right to hold men in bondage and slavery? We Yankees believe in freedom not slavery!" Who has the moral high ground in this debate? Facts are on our side but emotion is on our conquerors' side. In a democracy emotion trumps fact every time.

How do we take and hold the moral high-ground? We must go on the offensive and give them an argument and fight they are not accustomed to having to deal with and fight. Our argument is that we believe in Independence just like Americans in 1776—as noted in the Declaration of Independence. Attack "those people" for making economic and political slaves out of all Southerners; for systematically impoverishing ALL Southerners—an example is the per capita Millionaires in Mississippi. Thanks to Yankee invasion and occupation, Mississippi went from one of the richest states to one of the poorest states in the Union. As a result of Yankee victory, sharecropping became a new form of slavery in the South—both Black and White became enslaved. Of special interest is the fact that there were an equal number of families enslaved before and after the War. But after crushing the South, the system of slavery would include both White families as well as Black families; our counter-attack should include pointing out that the victors were maintaining their empire for the benefit of the ruling elite in Washington at the expense of the South—note that the richest counties in America, are around Washington, DC, New York City, and Hollywood.

The death knell for the Confederate flag, Southern heritage, and our liberty is assured by the continuation of a non-political, non-aggressive defense of our rights as Americans and Southerners. Where is OUR Charles Rangel? Where are our Rush Limbaughs rushing to attack our oppressors, those who have destroyed real American liberty? Where are our elected officials who will raise hell because of the Federal empire's abuse of our Rights as Americans?

Do these questions seem too radical? These questions are not just the fevered rantings of a latter-day neo-Confederate. The cruel and illegal conversion of these United States from a republic of republics into a unitary indivisible and supreme government, more akin to an empire than a free government, was predicted by a Northerner on the floor of the United States Senate in 1861. Warning Americans that Lincoln's war would destroy the sovereign states and replace it with a federal empire, Sen. Joseph Lane of Oregon said: "A province of an empire, how much so ever oppressed, is held by the oppressor as an integral part of his dominions. The yoke, once fastened on the neck of the subject, is expected, however galling, to be worn with patience and entire submission to the tyrant's will. This is the theory of despotism... when our Government was formed, our fathers fondly thought that they had made a great improvement on the despotic systems of modern Europe. They saw the infinite evil resulting from coercing the unwilling obedience of a subject to a Government which he abhorred and detested. They accordingly declared the great truth, never enunciated until then, that 'Governments derive all their just powers from the consent of the governed.' A Government without such consent they held to be a tyranny." Lane in 1861 was making the same argument against the use of force to "save the Union" as Edmond Burke made in the English Parliament in 1776. Burke warned his fellow Englishmen that the use of force against America would not only destroy the union [British and American Colonies] but it would also be an attack upon freedom itself. Burke noted by waging war upon the thirteen seceded American Colonies, England would "deprecate the idea of Freedom itself." He noted that "the thing you fought for [saving the union] is not the thing you recovered but deprecated, sunk, wasted and consumed in the contest." Both Burke in 1776 and Lane in 1861 were speaking from the moral high-ground.

Shortly after the defeat of the South, in a letter to his friend Lord Acton of Great Britain, Gen. Lee noted what would be the result of American government once real States' Rights were lost. Lee noted "I consider it [real States' Rights] as the chief source of stability to our political system, whereas the consolidation of the states into one vast republic, sure to be aggressive abroad and despotic at home, will be the certain precursor of that which has overwhelmed all those that have preceded it." General Lee understood the danger of living in a nation where "we the people" live for the benefit of the empire rather than the government living for the benefit of "we the people." In April of 1906, while speaking to the Sons of Confederate Veterans, General Stephen D. Lee issued his now famous "Charge:"

"To you, Sons of Confederate Veterans, we will commit the vindication of the Cause for which we fought. To your strength will be given the defense of the Confederate soldier's good name, the guardianship of his history, the emulation of his virtues, the perpetuation of those principles which he loved and which you love also, and those ideals which made him glorious and which you also cherish."

From the mouth of a Confederate Veteran, we virtually hear his request not for "reconciliation" but for "vindication!" Shortly after the close of World War I, a descendant of a Confederate Veteran and veteran of World War I offered these thoughts about "vindicating" the Cause of the South:

"In the South we are coming too much to whisper that 'our fathers did their duty as they saw it.' We should be calling to the world from the housetop that our Confederate fathers were right.... To be just to our Confederate fathers we must have a fuller grasp of the fundamental legal grounds and of the weighty causes which moved the South."

Thus, spoke Major E. W. R. Ewing, a descendant of a Confederate Veteran, a veteran of the United States Army, having served in action during WWI, and Historian-in-Chief of the Sons of Confederate Veterans. This American patriot did not hesitate to proclaim that "our Confederate fathers were right." He took the charge of General S. D. Lee seriously and worked to make sure that the principles upon which the Confederate States of America were founded were understood by the next generation of Americans. As Americans, Southerners should reject reconciliation if by that term Southerners are called upon to reject that form of government given to all Americans by America's Founding Fathers. Southerners must reject reconciliation if by that term it means that we must meekly accept our role as America's second-class economic and political citizens. Such status would reflect the condition of Americans under the tyranny of King George's government and not the status as a member of America's original Constitutional Republic of Republics. Patrick Henry correctly stated the issue when he proclaimed: "The first thing I have at heart is American liberty, the second is American union." Our founding fathers believed that in a free society, liberty always trumps government. Otherwise, as Senator Lane of Oregon warned America, Southerners and all other Americans will become subjects of an empire where, as General Robert E. Lee warned, we will become citizens of a nation that is "aggressive abroad and despotic at home."

General Lee once said that "Duty then is the most sublime word in the English language. Do your duty in all things, you cannot do more, one should never wish to do less." Our duty is to transfer to our children and their children the knowledge of the true history of our land so that they may do what others have not been able to do, that is, restore to this fair land that liberty which Patrick Henry noted was more important than life itself— "Give me liberty or give me death!" I hope to live to see the day when our Southland will have been, as Gen. Stephen D. Lee requested of the Sons of Confederate Veterans, **VINDICATED!** Oh, what a beautiful thought, oh what a blessed condition, when a generation of Southerners are born who will not have to apologize for their Southern accent or grow up in a nation that demands of them to sit upon the "stools of everlasting repentance!" Till that day comes, let us do our duty and pray this prayer, "The South, the grand, the glorious, the everlasting South, God Save the South!"

Chapter XIX

VINDICATING DIXIE'S YOUNG WARRIORS

IN MOST, IF NOT ALL SCV Camps, meetings are opened with a recitation of the Charge given to our organization by General Stephen D. Lee. When we speak of "vindicating the Cause" for which those veterans fought, we usually think of those men as old veterans. But those gray-haired veterans we see in photographs with an empty coat sleeve, missing a leg or leaning on a crutch, were once young and vigorous men. The War for Southern Independence, like all wars, was fought by men in their youthful prime. With their future before them (business, wife, children and a peaceful existence), for us they chose the uniform of a Confederate Soldier with its inherent danger.

The three photographs above will offer the reader a chance to look into the eyes of young Confederate Veterans. Notice the youthful, almost child-like, facial features of these young men. They were eagerly willing to leave home and all its comforts and security to defend their family and friends from the threats of a cruel invader. Fredrick Swint Hood joined the 28th La. Vol. Inf. at the young age of 16. He and the 28th La. Regiment played an important role in the defeat of the Yankee invader at the Battle of Mansfield, La. When I obtained his photograph, I was shocked to notice how much his great-great-great granddaughter looks like this man. You see, we Southerners have Confederate DNA! John J. Sitton of Missouri was 15 years old when he volunteered, serving first with the 4th Ark. Vol. Inf. and later with the Missouri State Guard. Levy Carnine joined the 2nd La. Vol. Inf., as a body guard for his master in 1861. When his master was killed in action during a battle in Virginia, Levy tended to his master's burial and rejoined the men of the 2nd La. Inf. After the fall of Vicksburg and Port Hudson, the Mississippi River being under the control of the invader and limiting contact to North Louisiana, Levy was asked to take on a dangerous mission. He was asked to take letters from the men of the 2nd La. back though Yankee controlled territory, cross the Mississippi River and deliver their letters to their families. Levy accepted the challenge and successfully brought the letters entrusted to him to the families of the men from North Louisiana.

After the War, Levy became an active member of the local United Confederate Veterans. Upon his death, his compatriots prepared his funeral but were told by some local individuals that Levy, "a colored man," could not be buried alongside the other Confederate Veterans in the community's "White" cemetery. The Confederate Veterans informed those individuals that Levy would be buried with all the Veterans. When faced with the resolute will of the old Confederate Veterans, common sense and goodwill prevailed. Today Levy's grave and all Confederate Veterans graves in Mansfield, La. are maintained by the Sons of Confederate Veteran.

Every time we repeat the Charge given to us by General Stephen D. Lee, let us remember not just the old veterans but the young men who gave up so much to defend our homeland and our Rights. Some gave their lives, some their health, but all gave up their youth to defend the South. As a result of Yankee invasion and conquest, all Southerners inherited a homeland laid waste, beset with poverty, and tormented with near starvation. Even under such dire circumstances, Southerners resolved to honor their heroes. During the celebration of the first annual Confederate Memorial at SCV National Headquarters, Past Commander-in-Chief Chuck McMichael noted that "Laurels of victory and honor were awarded our Confederate Veterans by a grateful Southland." Commander McMichael noted that such honors were based in the Graeco-Roman tradition and the Laurel Wreath today is seen on most Confederate Veteran tombstones. The Veterans did their duty, let us do our duty and properly honor them.

Victory in Arkansas

At the writing of this 'Forward the Colors,' news has been received about a double victory for the Cause of the South in Arkansas. The Arkansas Sons of Confederate Veterans were instrumental in successfully defeating a bill that would remove a holiday celebrating the Confederacy. Also, they assisted in the passage of a bill which protected all historical monuments, including Confederate monuments, signs, and placards. This victory is not the only such victory that has happened in the past few months. As was discussed in the April Commander's Comment video, several SCV Divisions have led the way to establishing laws to protect our heritage as well as turning back attacks upon Southern heritage. If you have not viewed April's Commander's Comment, please go to www.makedixiegreatagain.org and hear Commander McCluney's remarks on our success. But just as important as these local victories are, we must learn how to turn local victories into Confederation wide news.

Any victory for the Cause of the South needs to be spread across the South for two reasons. First, by reporting on a victory in one State, our members and the general public will be inspired to stand firm against neo-Marxist attacks in their State. Secondly, as news about our victories begin to spread, the political establishment will take notice.

What Do I Get For My $50?

I was recently told by a compatriot that his camp adjutant complained to him because he "never got anything" for his $50 membership in the Confederate Legion (CL). Here is what you get for your membership fee or donation to the CL In the past four months the CL secured radio ads on stations in the following States: Texas, Arkansas, Mississippi, Louisiana, and North Carolina; we have printed and distributed hundreds of copies of the Southern Defender; produced several pro-South videos, including four or more Commander's Comments; and maintained our social media outreach via Facebook and our Make Dixie Great Again website. When I say "created radio ads" or "printed and distributed" Southern Defenders, or produced videos, that means someone, a volunteer, had to start with nothing and develop an end product. We have to write and approve all ads, then have them professionally created so as to be usable by any number of radio stations. That's the easy part. Then we must contact a station and begin the negotiations to purchase air time, make payment, and maintain records that prove where our money is going. A similar set of events must take place with any project the Legion pursues. Please remember that from the start of this effort, we pledged that 90% of funds collected would be spent getting our pro-South message out to the general public. If you don't hear an ad or see a Southern Defender in your area, check with your camp. Most of the ads the CL runs are done in cooperation with a local camp. We will be delighted to work with any camp or division to assist in getting our SCV message aired or read in your area.

Recently an individual complained that he never hears anything from or about the Confederate Legion. When questioned, he stated that he had never read 'Forward the Colors' in any issue of the Confederate Veteran magazine, never opened his Confederate Legion Newsletter, never watched the monthly Commander's Comment, and did not know about MDGA Facebook or website. We need informed SCV members so they know not just how we are working for them, but most importantly, we need members who are up-to-date on what is going on and are ready to engage the enemy with knowledge and facts. Read the Confederate Veteran, get your camp involved in spreading the word about our noble heritage via the Southern Defender, promoting our videos on social media, and at least three or four times a year, purchase ads on a local radio station. Together we can "take back the narrative" from our neo-Marxist enemies.

THE SOUTH SHALL RISE AGAIN OR VAE VICTIS

The old truism "Much truth has been said in jest" holds true for the defeat of the South and the slogan "The South shall rise again!" Not long after the defeat and enslavement of the people of the Confederate States of America, many Southerners started jokingly repeating the slogan, "The South shall rise again." This slogan demonstrates our people's attempt to come to terms with the sad reality of defeat and foreign domination. This slogan also held out the hope that somehow, out of the ashes of defeat, the once free South could regain her rightful place as a free people. The idea of "vindicating the Cause for which they fought" is another example of looking to the future where the Cause of the South will be vindicated.

The Cause of the South can only be vindicated by the positive action of Southerners as we teach the children of the South the truth of our history and manfully proclaim to the world that "The South Was Right!" If today's generation of Southerners are not instructed in true Southern history and heritage, the South will ultimately suffer the Roman curse, Vae Victis. The simple translation of the Latin phrase, vae victis, is "woe to the victim" or "woe to the defeated." When a Roman army subdued a nation, that nation was looted of all its valuables, its culture was subverted for the good of Rome, and its people sold into slavery. The defeated was denied everything including hope. It is the job of the SCV to offer hope to the defeated so that vae victis will not become the refrain of tomorrow's Southland.

To spread the message of Southern Hope, three years ago the SCV established the Confederate Legion. It is the job of the Confederate Legion to create and distribute tools to be used by SCV camps to counter the negative publicity that is daily injected into American society. You and your Camp will be the ones who see to it that Deo Vindice, the motto on the Great Seal of the Confederacy, and not Vae Victis is the lot of the Southland of the future.

WALL STREET JOURNAL'S CONFEDERATE ANIMUS:

To truly vindicate the name and honor of the Confederate Veteran, we must insist that the truth be told. The lackies of political correctness will set up a howl and attack anyone, regardless of his credentials, when faced with the truth about Yankee invasion and occupation of the South. Thus, when historian, Dr. Samuel Mitcham's book on the Vicksburg Campaign was reviewed by the Wall Street Journal, the Yankee Empire went into full attack mode against Dr. Mitcham as noted in the following article.

As displayed in a review of Dr. Sandy Mitcham's book: *Vicksburg*

On the eve of the War for Southern Independence an article was published in *The New York Times* which unequivocally announced why the North had to invade and conquer the South. The author of the article declared, "The commercial bearing of the question has acted upon the North... . We were divided and confused [about Southern secession] till our pockets were touched." The Union Democrat of New Hampshire added this observation, "The Southern Confederacy will not employ our ships or buy our goods... . No—we must not 'let the South go.'" In an article titled "What Shall Be Done for a Revenue," the *Evening Post* of New York warned that without tariff income from Southern ports, "the sources which supply our treasury will be dried up... . the railways would be supplied from southern ports."

These three citations are a small representative sample of the numerous editorials by Northern newspapers warning of the dire consequences to Northern commerce and industry if the South was allowed to establish its independence. Rather than being the vaunted champion of freedom and equality, it is obvious that the worship of the "Almighty Dollar" was the driving force in the North's War to Prevent Southern Independence. Notice how the *Evening Post* of New York warned that Southern ports would be the recipient of railway commerce.

From early in the history of the Republic, the merchants of the Northeast lived with one great fear, losing its choke-hold on the nation's commerce. If the expanding nation's wealth flowed down the Mississippi River to the port of New Orleans and if Memphis became the hub for the nation's major railroads, commerce would flow into New Orleans and the ports along the Southern East Coast and Gulf South. This is why early in the Republic's history many Northeast merchants attempted to sell the Mississippi River to Spain (circa, 1779). Southern Historian, Francis Butler Simkins, noted the Yankee's "money grubbing" nature declaring, "Northern capitalism was eagerly imperialistic... its success was creating a nation of dollar-worshipers... who regarded themselves as the lords of creation." Empires are built and maintained by dollar-worshipers not by liberty-worshipers. According to James Madison, America's Founding Fathers did not create an Empire but created a compound republic. Lincoln, the Republican Party, and their crony-capitalist allies destroyed Madison and Jefferson's compound republic and replaced it with an ever-growing supreme Federal government—from which has sprung today's infamous Deep State. The South's long-standing love for States' Rights stood in the way of the North's desire for a commercial empire. Therefore, the South had to be destroyed. Today, anyone who dares to proclaim any view that does not comport with the view of the Empire is assaulted in the well-used and jaded method of ridicule and questioning of one's "historical credentials." And if the Empire can produce a self-loathing Southerner who, like Judas, is willing to betray his people for a few Yankee coins, it makes the Empire's work of defending invasion and oppression much easier.

Recently the *Wall Street Journal (WSJ) published* a review of Dr. Sandy Mitcham's book, *Vicksburg*. The first portion of the review gave credit to Dr. Mitcham for his work but from that point forward a virtual anti-South tirade flows from the reviewer's keyboard. The reviewer insists that Dr. Mitcham's arguments and quotes are not properly "sourced" as is expected for "scholarly history." A Southern historian or writer can barricade himself up to his eyeballs in "citations," "references," "primary source materials," and it will do little to placate the running dogs and lackeys of political correctness. Traditional Southerners understand that any book which does not "tow-the-line" of the Empire's view of the War will never be accepted as "scholarly." The *WSJ* reviewer condemns Dr. Mitcham's work on five broad grounds. (1) He claims that Mitcham's maps are "sparse and sketchy." Perhaps Dr. Mitcham understood that facts about the human element such as death, starvation, and terrorism inflicted on Southern civilians by the invader were of more interest and more important than "un-sketchy" maps. (2) The reviewer found fault with Mitcham's description of Grant as "desperate." After unsuccessfully attempting to take Vicksburg four times, Grant was indeed becoming desperate. It was Grant who had over 7000 of his men killed trying desperately to break Lee's fortifications at Cold Harbor. Grant understood that it takes desperate measures to defeat men who are defending their homes and families from a cruel invader. (3) The *WSJ* reviewer was somewhat incredulous that Dr. Mitcham would condemn Sherman for his "overbearing cruelty." Sherman, who suggested to the Federal Empire's War Department that a whole class of Southerners "men, women, and children should be killed or banished" to secure victory is given a "get out of jail free" card by the reviewer. (4) Mitcham's view of Lincoln is also condemned. Lincoln, the man who had the civilian grandson of Francis Scott Key arrested, tried, and jailed by military police and given a military trial, is not one who should be given a pass when looking for tyrants! (5) Mitcham's refusal to kowtow to the Empire's god of political correctness was more than the *WSJ* reviewer could tolerate, especially as it relates to slavery!

As Henrik Ibsen noted in *An Enemy of the People*, "You should never wear your best trousers when you go out to fight for freedom and truth." I can assure you that Dr. Mitcham had his fighting clothes on when he wrote *Vicksburg*. As a well-trained and honest historian, Dr. Mitcham abhors political correctness and its sycophants. Nevertheless, it is understandable why the *WSJ* would publish a review which criticizes Dr. Mitcham's book; after all, no one has more to lose from exposing the lies, myths, and falsehoods which prop up the Yankee Empire than Wall Street. Yankees and their sycophants will never understand Dr. Mitcham's view on the War because they do not understand that a conquered people never forget!

Chapter XX

SEE, WE TOLD Y'ALL SO!

DURING THE PAST TEN YEARS, many members and leaders of the SCV have warned the American public of the danger of allowing neo-Marxist radicals a free hand in their attack upon all things Confederate. Starting three years ago the Commander-in-Chief and Chief of Heritage Operations have repeated the warning about neo-Marxist attacks during the monthly Commander's Comments. Over and over, it has been stressed that it's not just Confederate heritage that is under attack but actually, its Traditional American Values that are under attack. The attack upon the Confederacy was just the first phase of the neo-Marxist's attack upon Traditional American Values. Attacking our Southern heritage and the honoring our Confederate ancestors was merely the neo-Marxists' test-run for attacking Traditional American Values. Today more than ever, we are witnessing the result of their successful effort.

Where once it was only the Confederate flag that was stigmatized and attacked, currently the thirteen star "Betsy Ross" United States flag as well as all other flags of the War for American independence, such as the Gadsden flag, are being condemned as racists' emblems. Neo-Marxists hammered out a successful template by stigmatizing the Confederate flag and monuments as racist, they then moved on to attacking the United States flags and heroes. Recently, monuments to Theodore Roosevelt, William McKinley (a Union Veteran), the Oregon Trail Pioneers, Columbus, and many others have been removed due to neo-Marxist pressure—see, we told y'all so! During the past July 4th celebration two monuments were attacked and desecrated. At the Manassas National Battlefield Park, the monument honoring General Stonewall Jackson was smeared with a coating of red and yellow paint, while in Asheville, NC, a statue of Jesus was smeared with red paint and a portion broken. If one ever needed proof that the same cabal of leftist thugs who hate the South also hate all traditional American values, here is the proof.

Unfortunately, the beautiful city of Asheville, NC, has been inundated with left-wing loons who now appear to have taken over this once beautiful Southern city. Asheville is the same city that kowtowed to neo-Marxists by having the impressive statue of Governor Zebulon Vance removed. Way to go Asheville, first a pro-Confederate Governor's monument is removed and then a statue of Jesus is desecrated by leftist loons. The radicals who attack Christ and Stonewall Jackson will not stop until everything of traditional value is destroyed—it is not just the Confederate flag they are after. In a recent article, singer/actor Macy Gray stated "Gimme a New U.S. Flag!!!" In an op-ed posted in 'MarketWatch,' Gray wrote that Old Glory needed a face lift because it is "tattered, dated, divisive, and incorrect" and the reviewer of her op-ed added "just like the Confederate flag." Gray opined that modern America has changed and "it's time for a reset, a transformation." Notice the last word in that sentence, "transformation." As we have said from the start, what the left is after is a complete make-over of these United States, not just Southern heritage. Representative Maxine Waters took to her social media during the July 4th celebration and condemned the Declaration of Independence as a virtual "white supremacist document." If these actions were just isolated, non-recurring actions and statements, they could be laughed at and ignored. The past fifty years of ignoring these radicals has led to the current round of anti-Confederate and anti-Traditional American Values success. As we push our educational projects always remember that we are seeking to influence John Q. Public and not attempting to convert radical loons. The radicals have already rejected the truth. Radicals do not reject the truth because of lack of evidence but because they hate the truth. Because we are representatives of the truth, neo-Marxists will hate Christians, Southerners, and all Americans holding Traditional American Values.

What is taking place in America today is very similar to what took place during the Cultural Revolution in Communist China from 1966 to 1976. The Cultural Revolution was initiated on the order of the communist ruler of China, Mao Zedong. Mao's Red

Guards stated they would destroy and replace the four "olds," that is, old ideas, old culture, old habits, and old traditions. During the Communist Cultural Revolution in China, mobs destroyed grave sites and family genealogical records; the remains of dead heroes were exhumed, desecrated and disposed of; monuments were torn down; and thousands of people became targets of mob and governmental harassment and even death. It has been estimated that by the end of this communist revolution as many as one million people had been murdered by Mao Zedong's radicals.

Look at the four olds the communists of China were attacking as it relates to the attack upon the South and traditional American values. Old ideas: The old and once acknowledged idea that Confederate Veterans and Southern history would be respected has been under attack for over 30 years. Old culture: The Biblical world view that was once recognized and respected by the vast majority of Americans is now the object of ridicule and desecration. The desecration of the statue of Jesus in Asheville, NC, is just the most recent of such attacks. Old habits: The habit of love of family and community with respect for the opinions of others is not acceptable in the eyes of neo-Marxists. Old traditions: As the SCV has been warning our fellow Americans, all Traditional American Values are under attack by the same enemies who are attacking all things Confederate. The traditional love for the Constitution, Declaration of Independence and flags of the United States- Betsy Ross, Gadsden, and the current U. S. flag, are all now under attack. We are witnessing the destruction of traditional American patriotism and its replacement with a demand of loyalty to a "woke," un-American socialist state. Because the political and cultural establishment would not allow us a fair chance to tell the truth about Southern history and culture, the neo-Marxists gained a foothold in American culture and they are using that foothold to attack all Traditional American Values.

As a health care professional, I have had friends whose life-style and choices were not conducive to a long life. I would plead and argue with them and warn them of the imminent danger they were facing to no avail. As I visited their graves, it was never fun to say "I told you so!" Likewise, upon viewing all these attacks upon traditional American values, it is not fun to tell our fellow Americans, "I told you so!" This is not the time for recrimination but the time to double our efforts to get our message of truth about the South to our fellow Americans in general and our fellow Southerners in particular.

If we who love the South and Traditional American Values are to survive, what must we do? We must go on the offensive. For too long the SCV has been reactive. We spend our time reacting to the enemy's attack. It's time to make them react to our actions. The struggle we are engaged in today is essentially a public relations struggle. Therefore, we must place our message in front of the general public (educate) thereby encouraging them to remain loyal to Southern heritage (motivate) and recruit warriors to assist in this struggle (activate).

Since flags, monuments, and cemeteries cannot tell the truth about our history, heritage, and culture, we must be their voice. Cleaning Confederate tombstones is a noble project but a clean stone will not convince the unknowing about the nobility of our beloved dead. A giant Confederate flag is inspiring to those who understand the truth about that flag but to the unknowing, the only narrative they understand is that narrative told them by leftist media, academia and other left-wing propogandists. Unless we tell the truth about that flag and the Cause of the South, future viewers of that flag will despise it as a hate-filled rag. We must tell the truth, take back the narrative, or this and worse will be the lot for Southern heritage.

Three years ago, the SCV established the Confederate Legion (CL) to be our primary instrument for taking our message to the general public. Think of this effort as a public relations operation—our "narrative" verses the enemy's "narrative." We are in a business; we sell CORRECT Southern history. Our product, if embraced by our fellow Southerners, will destroy the false neo-Marxist narrative about the South. Not only will it prevent Southerners from abandoning the Cause of the South but it will force the political establishment to treat Southern heritage fairly.

Every two months the CL sponsors a Confederate Counter-Attack. Each attack has a positive theme about the South. Each theme is supported by CL produced radio ads, videos and letters to be sent to community leaders and organizations, as well as copies of the Southern Defender. Every SCV Camp is encouraged to join in these Confederate Counter-Attacks and tell our neighbors about why they should be proud of their heritage. Think of these CL tools as your weapons to defeat the neo-Marxists in your community. By using these weapons in your community, your camp makes the first phase of total Southern Victory possible. Education in the form of positive information, given in various and continuous ways, will create a positive feeling for the Southern Cause and begin the process of total victory for the Cause of the South.

Because of the lack of a strong pro-South message going forth in our local community, the political establishment has no fear nor remorse in joining forces with the neo-Marxists to destroy Sothern heritage. Recently 67 "conservative" members of the United States House of Representatives voted along with their liberal colleagues to remove all statues of "Confederate" heroes in the U.S. Capitol. One such "conservative" was a representative from one of the most conservative districts in Louisiana, yet he had no fear of joining the BLM/Antifa jihad against Southern heritage. Until the SCV becomes a well-known organization within our communities, this will only get worse. Don't be fooled into thinking these neo-Marxist radicals will stop at just taking down a few monuments. Their ultimate objective is the utter destruction of all semblance and remembrance of the South. I have heard these neo-Marxist radicals say that they will not stop until the names of all Southern States have been changed to "un-hurtful" names and the bodies of all racist traitors, i.e., Confederate Veterans, are exhumed and disposed of. We are in a fight for our very existence. But doing the same thing we have been doing for the past thirty years will not lead to victory.

Thirty years ago, when the Kennedy Twins predicted the coming campaign of cultural genocide, we were ridiculed and condemned as too radical and too pessimistic— "after all, this is America, we have the Constitution to protect us" is what we were told. Our predictions and warnings have come true but there is no pleasure in saying, "I told y'all so!" Let us go forward today with renewed vigor, retake lost ground and totally defeat our enemies, "or that little upon which we now barely subsist upon will surely be taken from us."

SECESSION: FOUNDATION OF AMERICAN FREEDOM

Most politically perceptive Americans are beginning to understand that ALL Traditional American Values are under attack. Everything from traditional moral, i.e., Christian, standards to even the National Anthem are subject to being either banned or "reinterpreted" according to the neo-Marxist myth. But where did this process begin? It began with the destruction of Real States' Rights, the foundation for the American Right of secession.

"The presidential election... showed that America is now divided..." This remark was not made in response the Trump/Biden election of 2020 but rather, the Bush/Gore 2000 presidential election. Although twenty years apart, both elections prove that the United States was and is in reality the Disunited States of America. In the aftermath of the 2000 election there were sweeping calls for secession from the political left. In 2000, journalist Peter Applebome, writing in the *New York Times*, suggested that in light of the (2000) election the option of secession should be taken seriously. Now fast forward 20 years and with the debacle of the 2020 presidential election, again we hear and read calls for secession—but this time the calls were from both the political right and left.

When conservative mega talk-show host Rush Limbaugh [this was written before the unfortunate death of Mr. Limbaugh] mentioned that he had heard many people proposing secession and admitted that the nation was much divided, the talk and calls for secession exploded on social media. Limbaugh mentioned that yes indeed America was a divided nation so much so that, "There cannot be a peaceful coexistence of two completely different theories of government... ." As he correctly observed, this conflict of opposing philosophies of government cannot coexist. One philosophy must triumph over the other, which of course means that one philosophy will have to be *suppressed*. It is at this point that Limbaugh said that it appears that America was trending in the direction of secession. Limbaugh never said he was in favor of secession. Nevertheless, the fact that he mentioned secession and admitted that the country was tragically polarized into two near warring camps, caused an explosion in the conversation about secession. Limbaugh, who has a history of ridiculing those who called his radio show supporting the right of secession, had let slip the "dogs of war" for secession!

That which many today believe is un-American, i.e., secession, was a concept that was taken for granted as legitimate for the first 84 years of the history of these United States of America (1776 to 1860). Even though the idea of the right of secession today is not embraced by the majority of Americans, that number favoring the right of secession is growing. Why would secession be more acceptable today than fifty years ago? Two big reasons have caused this change in attitude about secession; size and philosophy. At the adoption of the Constitution in 1788, the election of delegates to the House of Representatives was the primary means for the people of the States to impact or *interact* with the Federal government. At that time the number of citizens in each congressional district was set at 40,000 per representative. Today that number is around 600,000 citizens per representative. Few citizens feel like their voice can be heard, let alone responded too, by such a big, far-away central government. Recent polls have demonstrated that faith in the Federal government is at an all-time low of 17%, which is lower than faith in used-car salesmen. The second reason secession is more embraced and therefore, more probable today, is divergent philosophies of how a government should interact with the people.

At one time the philosophical divide in America was simply a contest of small government verses big government. Small government conservatives and big government liberals could work together for common goals and not feel as if their very liberty was in danger because of an opponent's election victory. Today that has changed. Each side now views the other side as a deadly enemy. Liberals feel that if their big-government projects such as climate change, environmental laws, sexual equality laws, income equality, and such are not enacted, the world will come to an end. Therefore, for the good of humanity, those who stand in their way, i.e., advocates of small government, must be destroyed. For small government conservatives, they see liberals are destroying the very essence of the American dream and freedom itself. Conservatives see big-government advocates as enemies of individual rights and property. Liberals, advocating the forceful transferring of wealth from the productive (tax-paying) citizens to the non-productive (tax-consuming) element of society, are viewed as an attack upon the very foundation of the Republic. Conservatives warn that the liberal on-rush to standardize equality via mass democracy is the very thing America's Founding Fathers warned us against. It is at that point that government will have been reduced to an instrument of legalized plunder and that plunder will surely extend to the liberty and freedom of every American. Thus, if like Patrick Henry we love liberty more than government, we cannot live in a nation where that philosophy rules. When such a point is reached, the plundered will seriously consider secession.

Patrick Henry pointed the way for all freedom-loving people when faced with the choice of seceding from perceived tyranny or remaining loyal to the existing government when he stated: "The first thing I have at heart is American liberty, the second thing is American union." As America's Founding Fathers noted in the Declaration of Independence, people have an unalienable right to "alter or abolish" any government that they no longer respect. This concept is known as the American principle of "government by the consent of the governed." This principle puts "we the people" in charge of the government and not the government in charge of "we the people." Thus, the Right of Secession is not only very American, it is absolutely necessary if we are to be a free people.

Chapter XXI

THE THREE PHASES OF SOUTHER VICTORY
James R. Kennedy

NO CONSERVATIVE ORGANIZATION, Southern heritage organization, or the "conservative" Republican Party has ever developed a strategic plan to defeat America's neo-Marxist enemies. None of these organizations can define what the ultimate victory would look like, much less how to achieve that victory. We go from one dismal political defeat to another thinking "well, we'll do better the next time." At the rate we are going as a nation—we are fast approaching the moment when there will not be "another time."

We must recognize that Southerners and non-Southerners in Red State and Red County America are a stateless people. We have no government that will actively protect and (more importantly) actively promote our interests. Stateless people are political slaves to the country's ruling elites. For those pacified "conservatives" who think they are safe because they have "their" state government and a federal government limited by the Constitution—the following two examples should cause them to question their confidence. These are just two examples of Americans as stateless people. Statelessness example one: The people of California passed a statewide ballot initiative that made the definition of marriage as between one man and one woman but the federal government nullified the will of the people. Statelessness example two: The people of Mississippi voted in a statewide ballot initiative to

> **"We the people"** are a stateless people! We are the ruling elites' political slaves. **Political slaves** are easy targets for genocide.

keep their traditional state flag but the Republican governor and Republican legislature, following the instructions of their Deep State masters, met in a rump session and overruled the will of the people. We are the political slaves of America's leftist, ruling elites. America's ruling elites' utter disdain and contempt for "We the people" is shown when they refer to us as "deplorables," "irredeemables," and "bitter clingers." Political slaves are easy targets for cultural, and ultimately, actual genocide. This will be the fate of the South if "We the people" of Dixie remain passive subjects of the supreme federal government.

> **Provisional Governments in every American Red State and Red County will use irregular political warfare to force the neo-Marxists who control the Federal Government to recognize our right of local self-government or, if necessary, the right of self-determination.**

A strategic plan to defeat America's woke, politically correct, ruling elite is outlined in *Dixie Rising: Rules for Rebels*.[1] The book explains how to conduct irregular political warfare. It also documents five occupied nations that used irregular political warfare to gain their independence or, at least, they forced their central government to respect their heritage and natural rights.

America's Constitutional government can be reclaimed! It can be done if we have the courage and audacity to implement the strategic plan explained in *Dixie Rising: Rules for Rebels*. The key elements of the plan are: (1) the establishment of Provisional governments in every Southern County and State and every non-Southern Red State or Red County, (2) using the Provisional government organized at the county level to support—and if necessary to enforce—the lobbying efforts in the state legislature. This will be done by using the political clout gained by grassroots, active, Provisional governments bringing pressure on weak-kneed, elected officials. We will also use this power to force

---

1 Kennedy, James Ronald, *Dixie Rising: Rules for Rebels*, 2nd edition (Columbia, SC: Shotwell Publishing, 2021).

Congress to submit to the States the Sovereign State Amendment.[2] The Sovereign State Amendment acknowledges the Sovereign State's rights of nullification and secession.

The key to "jump-starting" this movement is to elect one of our own to a statewide office—someone who will use that office as a Bully Pulpit to promote the establishment of Provisional governments across the South and Red State/Red County America. The Bully Pulpit must be held by one of our own, NOT a "good" conservative politician. He must be someone with a strategic plan who is dedicated to the movement of reclaiming America's original, Constitutionally limited Republic of Sovereign States—the original American government that Lincoln and the Republican Party destroyed.

This is a choice between liberty or continued political slavery. Our past failures were a result of grassroots conservatives depending on business-as-usual political efforts. If we keep doing what we have always done we will find ourselves—in the words of John Randolph, "The little on which we now subsist will be taken from us." The choice is yours—but remember time is running out!

---

2 A copy of the Sovereign State Amendment can be found at bit.ly/sovereignty-ammendment.

Recognizing The South's Historical Strategic Failure

The South's social and political failure is proven by a simple recitation of the slanderous attacks that have been successfully made against us. (1) The massive destruction of Confederate monuments, (2) the renaming of Military Bases named in honor of Confederate military leaders, (3) the slanderous excuses used by the Federal Congress to remove Southern monuments from the U.S. Capitol, (4) slanderously branding those who honor their Southern heritage as white supremacists, and (5) forcing Southerners to allow those who hate us to define our Southern heritage. Southerners are the only group in America who are not allowed to define their culture! These and many other acts of anti-Southern, cultural genocide are being successfully implemented because Southerners have never acknowledged our post-War strategic failure as a society. What are those post-War strategic failures?

First: Failure to clearly establish in the hearts and minds of each generation of Southerners that the South was fighting for freedom while the North was fighting for empire, and failing to continually press that point worldwide.

> • Post-War and up until the 1970s most Southerners were taught that the South fought for honorable principles but we failed to assign evil to the invader. As a society we were too polite to call attention to the crimes and poverty intentionally inflicted upon the South by the post-War Yankee Empire.

Second: Failure to continually denounce the post-War federal and state governments forced upon the Southern people as illegitimate governments—governments based not upon the Southern people's free and unfettered consent but governments based upon cruel military and political coercion.

> • We failed to constantly point out to our own people and to the world at large that the post-Reconstruction governments imposed upon the South violated the principle of "consent of the governed." We failed to understand that "our" state governments were no more

than mere puppet governments that were compelled to follow the rulings, legislation, and regulations enacted by the Yankee Empire. Similar to the way Ireland, before its independence, was forced to follow the will of the English Empire. This is the fate of all conquered people. Our problem was that, unlike the Irish, Southerners refused to admit that we are a conquered people. Our society became malleable clay in the hands of evil neo-Marxists who molded and established their definition of the South as the generally accepted definition of the War and the post-War Southern society.

Third: Failure to boldly point out to rising generations of Southerners and to the world the radical difference between States' Rights under America's original Constitution and states' privileges as allowed to the states under the radically and illegally altered (current) constitution.

- Lincoln and the Republican Party are the founding fathers of the current Yankee Empire. The original Constitution as advocated by the Founding Fathers and ultimately given life by the voluntary ratification of America's Sovereign States did not allow for a supreme federal government. The limitations and protections inscribed in the Constitution are ultimately enforced by the Sovereign State(s) as described by Thomas Jefferson and James Madison in the Kentucky and Virginia Resolutions of 1798. The current Constitution is a bayonet constitution put in place without the consent of "We the people" of the once sovereign states.

- The Constitution is NOT self-enforcing! "We the people" have been stripped of the political power, via our Sovereign States, to enforce the limitations on federal authority as allowed by the original Constitution. We are a stateless people—we have no government that will protect and (more importantly) actively promote our values and interests. As stateless people, we are political slaves to the neo-Marxist elites who control Lincoln's supreme federal government.

Fourth: Failure to recognize Lincoln's unconstitutional, supreme federal government as an enemy of true American constitutional government and liberty.

- None of the issues that conservatives complain about today would be possible in America's original, Constitutionally-limited Republic of Sovereign States. Abortion, gun-control, illegal immigration, and endless, no-win wars—all, and many others, have resulted from Lincoln's and the Republican Party's destruction of America's original and legitimate Republic of Sovereign States.

Fifth: Failure to acknowledge that the South is a captive nation—a people held and exploited by an outside power against the Southern people's will and in violation of the international principle of self-determination of people and nations.

- "We the people" of Dixie have no government that we can rely upon to consistently protect, and more importantly, to promote our social, moral, and political values. We are a stateless people! Citizens of a captive nation are always a stateless people. Stateless people are political slaves to their conquering masters.

Sixth: Failure to recognize the inherent horrors inflicted upon people of the world via the post-War, globalists Yankee Empire.

- General Lee made it plain in a letter to Lord Action when he predicted that if "those people" (Yankees) use their victory to destroy States' Rights then the United States would become "aggressive abroad and despotic at home."[3]

---

3   For detailed documentation of the Yankee Empire being "aggressive abroad," see, Kennedy & Kennedy, *Yankee Empire: Aggressive Abroad and Despotic at Home* (Columbia, SC: Shotwell Publishing, 2018).

Seventh: Failure to consistently and continually, over generations, demand Freedom and Independence for the South.

> • The South was right in 1861 because the American Colonies were right in 1776. The principle of self-determination of people did not change from 1776 to 1861! But, the Declaration of Independence was, in principle and practice, nullified by Lincoln and the Republican Party.

> • As described in *Dixie Rising: Rules for Rebels*, the valid threat of secession, in most cases, will cause an oppressive central government to reconsider its evil intentions against an occupied people. Unfortunately, Southerners meekly threw away this excellent bargaining position. But to be valid, the threat must be backed up by an honest intent to secede IF the oppressive government refuses to relent in its illegal oppressions.

As proponents of Constitutional liberty and defenders of our honorable, Southern heritage we must begin the effort to overcome our past strategic failure. The first step for proponents of our Southern heritage is to become local agents of influence for our Cause.

Since flags, monuments, and cemeteries cannot tell the truth about our history and culture, we must be their voice. The SCV established the Confederate Legion (CL) to be our primary way of taking our message to the general public. Think of this effort as a public-relations operation—our "narrative" verses the enemy's "narrative." We are a business; we offer the general public CORRECT Southern history. Our product if embraced by our fellow Southerners will destroy the neo-Marxists' false narrative about the South. Not only will it prevent Southerners from abandoning the Cause of the South, it will force the political establishment to treat Southern heritage fairly.

Phase 1: Reach Out to Our Natural Supporters

The weapons we use are the tools of any good public-relations, marketing, or "propaganda" effort. We must place our message before the general public. Every other month the CL will launch a different "Confederate Counter-Attack." These six Counter-Attacks are as follows: (1) Confederate Diversity, (2) Confederate Veterans are American Veterans, (3) Religion in the Confederacy, (4) July 4th Secession Holiday, (5) South's Defense of the Constitution, (6) Southern Thanksgiving and Christmas.

Each Counter-Attack is supported by videos, articles, radio and print ads. These "tools" for the Counter-Attack can be placed on camp and members social media. Additionally, every Counter-Attack will have a sample letter for your camp to use to contact civic and political leaders in your community asking them to view and read our message on You-tube and our website.

Using these weapons in your community, your camp will make Phase 1 of the Southern Victory effort possible. From Phase 1, we will move to the Phase 2 and ultimate victory in Phase 3. NOTE: This effort will not eliminate the SCV's traditional 501(c) (3) status.

Phase 2: Political Education and Lobbying

Phase 2 of SCV activity is conducted via IRS Rule 501(c)(4) which is separate from the SCV's 501(c)(3) activities. Donations to 501(c)(3) organizations are tax deductible. Donations to the SCV's 501(c)(4) political-education arm are not tax deductible. Money donated to the SCV's political-education arm can be used to support social causes and to publish facts about issues or correct slanderous statements about the SCV and our Cause.

IRS 501(c)(4) organizations engage in educating the community. Generally, political educational organizations must conduct their activities in a non-partisan manner. Such educational organizations may also engage in substantial lobbying activities.

SCV community, educational activities include activities such as: commissioning polling of the local public regarding issues pertaining to the maintenance of our Confederate monuments; sharing the results of public opinion polls with the public and local elected officials; and sponsoring lectures/videos urging voters to support any candidate who defends our Southern heritage. Lobbying efforts will secure the passage of laws requiring fair and balanced instruction in public schools and universities regarding the War for Southern Independence and making it a crime to accuse individuals of racism merely because they seek to honor their ancestors who served the Confederate States of America.

PHASE 3: TAKING DECISIVE POLITICAL ACTION

In Phase 3 members work outside of the SCV to gain political clout. Phase 3 is conducted by Southern-Heritage activists in conjunction with other American-values folks. Traditional American Values folks include Southern Heritage advocates, Second Amendment-rights advocates, traditional Christians who wish to promote traditional Christian values and Tea Party folks who wish to limit the size and taxing power of government. SCV members in conjunction with other American-values folks will establish a working group that will force the federal government, and when necessary, the state government, to protect and promote Traditional American Values.

Phase 3 is where "we the people" force the political establishment to honor our values. We do this by engaging in irregular political warfare. Phase 3 is the point in which we elect one of our own to a statewide political office. This elected official will use his office as a Bully Pulpit to arouse the general public across the nation and initiate a peaceful conservative revolution in which "we the people" will reclaim the right of local self-government. We will restore America's original Constitutional Republic—a Republic where the Constitution is enforced by "we the people" via the American rights of nullification and secession. Together we will make a fundamental change in America's current leftist government.

Slanderous Anti-South Legislation in U.S. House of Representatives

On August 10, 2021, New York Rep. Adriano Espaillat with 35 cosponsors introduced H.R. 4994. The official title is: H.R.4994 'No Federal Funding for Confederate Symbols Act' 117th Congress (2021-2022).

They justify the proposed prohibition on the use of Federal funds for any Confederate symbol because:

> The Congress finds the following:
>
> (1) The Confederate battle flag is one of the most controversial symbols from U.S. history, signifying a representation of racism, slavery, and the oppression of African Americans.
>
> (2) The Confederate flag and the erection of Confederate monuments were used as symbols to resist efforts to dismantle Jim Crow segregation, and have become pillars of Ku Klux Klan rallies.
>
> (3) There are at least 1,503 symbols of the Confederacy in public spaces, including 109 public schools named after prominent Confederates, many with large African-American student populations.
>
> (4) There are more than 700 Confederate monuments and statues on public property throughout the country, the vast majority in the South. These include 96 monuments in Virginia, 90 in Georgia, and 90 in North Carolina.

Every SCV member should contact his U.S. Representative asking them to vote against H.R. 4994 because of its hateful and slanderous misrepresentation of Southerners, past and present. The Bill was referred to the Subcommittee on Water Resources and Environment; the Subcommittee on Railroads, Pipelines, and Hazardous Materials; the Subcommittee on Highways and Transit; the Subcommittee on Economic Development, Public Buildings, and Emergency

Management; and the Subcommittee on Aviation. At this time (Aug. 21, 2021) no further action has been taken by the House.

If your congressman is on one of the subcommittees listed—it is especially important that you contact him and voice your opposition to the bill. Even if your congressman is not on one of these subcommittees—contact them and voice your opposition to the bill.

Stress that this bill will have a detrimental impact on Southern "Civil War" tourism.

James Ronald Kennedy

Mandeville, Louisiana

August 21, 2021 [Information obtained at https://www.congress.gov/]

Chapter XXII

THE FORGOTTEN 11ᵀᴴ AMENDMENT

FEW AMERICANS will dispute the suggestion that as a general rule, Americans are woefully ignorant regarding the United States Constitution. Yet, there are many professionals who study and cite the Constitution. Professionals such as attorneys, journalists, politicians, educators and media talking heads appear to have a much greater grasp upon the particulars of the Constitution than the general public. This does not mean that each individual holds a correct view of the Constitution nor do they agree with each other on Constitutional issues. While this group of enlightened Constitutional commentators will talk or write enthusiastically on the Constitution and especially on the First, Second, Fourth, and Tenth Amendments, the Eleventh Amendment is generally ignored. Let me ask this question: When was the last time you considered or read the Eleventh Amendment to the Constitution? Don't be embarrassed to say never or very seldom, after all, that would be the answer provided by the vast majority of even the "enlightened" Constitutional commentators.

Why is very little information written or spoken about the Eleventh Amendment? The Eleventh Amendment was the very first amendment added to the Constitution after the ratification of the Bill of Right. Is this amendment just an old antiquated addition to the Constitution and therefore of no modern value? Or is there something about this amendment that is so dangerous to today's power elites that Americans must be kept in the dark about its history?

No part of the Constitution, including any amendment, is time limited, otherwise freedom of speech, religion and association can be said to be too "old fashioned" and therefore of no value. But there is a very good reason why the Eleventh Amendment is little studied and discussed today. More than any other portion of the Constitution, the Eleventh Amendment completely invalidates and repudiates Lincoln and the Republican Party's reason for waging war upon the Confederate States of America.

In February of 1793, a mere five years after the adoption of the Constitution, the Federal Supreme Court handed down a decision in *Chisholm v. Georgia*.[4] This decision set the new nation in an uproar. A British creditor enlisted the aid of two South Carolina citizens to sue the State of Georgia to recover money owed to a British company. It must be noted that this was not a case where one State is suing another State but private citizens attempting to sue a State. The case went directly to the Supreme Court which, according to the Constitution, has original jurisdiction.[5] The State of Georgia refused to appear before the Court maintaining that a sovereign state cannot be compelled to appear anywhere it does not choose. The State of Georgia then nullified the Supreme Court decision and stated that any Federal agent that entered Georgia and attempted to enforce any portion of the Supreme Court decision, "shall be...declared to be guilty of felony, and shall suffer death, without benefit of clergy, by being hanged."[6] Constitutional scholar, Dr. Forrest McDonald, noted that when the Supreme Court announced the Chisholm decision, "Waves of protest swept the country."[7] At that time in American history, Americans understood that each State in the Union was a sovereign State and could not be compelled to act against its will. The key to understanding this conflict is understanding the nature of the term "sovereign."

A noted nineteenth century legal scholar, Francis Lieber, defines sovereignty thusly, "Sovereignty is the ability to execute any thought

---

4   *Chisholm v. Georgia*, 2 Dallas 419 (1793).

5   Article III, Section 2 United States Constitution.

6   Herman V. Ames, *State Documents on Federal Relations* (Philadelphia: Northeastern University Press, 1911), 10.

7   Forrest McDonald, *A Constitutional History of the United States* (Malabar, FL: Robert E. Krieger Publishing Co., 1982), 50.

or idea without limitation."⁸ From a theological viewpoint we can be assured that only God is Sovereign but from a political viewpoint sovereignty resides in the agency of government. The 16th century French political scholar, Jean Bodin (1530-1596), explains sovereignty as the "absolute and perpetual power of the state, that is, the greatest power to command."⁹ Bodin recognizes sovereignty as something that resides with a state due to its independent nature. According to Bodin, the state and the government are not the same. The government exists because a sovereign state calls it into existence. In America's original Union, "we the people" created our state government. "We the people" compose a sovereign community (State) and the people of that community create their State government. Therefore, it is the people, en masse, of that community who are sovereign, not the State government. Sovereignty is the ability to exercise supreme political power over a particular territory (State).

The Swiss political philosopher and diplomat, Emmerich de Vattel, asserted that regardless of the form of government, "Every nation that governs itself...without any dependence on foreign powers, is a sovereign State. Its rights are naturally the same as those of any other State."¹⁰ When looking at the history of the representation in the Continental Congress and the act of voting for independence it is obvious that each State, regardless of size, population, or wealth, is treated with absolute equality. Every State had one vote, as Vattel notes, "Its rights are naturally the same as those of any other State." This is reflected in the Constitution's equal representation for each State in the Senate. When called upon to elect the president, the House of Representatives will vote by State, each State having only one vote. This equality of the States is a reflection of the sovereign nature of the States as recognized by America's Founding Fathers.

So now we come to the question of where does sovereignty reside in these United States? Does sovereignty reside with the

---

8   Francis Lieber, *On Civil Liberty and Self Government* (Philadelphia: J.B. Lippincott and Co., 1853), 270.

9   Jean Bodin as cited in, William Ebenstein, ed., *Great Political Thinkers: Plato to the Present* (New York: Holt, Rinehart and Wilson, 1960), III, 349.

10 Emmerich de Vattel, *Laws of Nations* 6th ed. (1758, Philadelphia: T. & J.W. Johnson, Law Booksellers, 1844), I, 2.

politicians and judges of the Federal government, i.e., the Union, or does it reside with "we the people" of each sovereign State? If Americans are allowed to have a correct understanding of the history of the Eleventh Amendment, they may begin to question Lincoln and the Republican Party's destruction of the original Union and therefore, the Constitution. Lincoln's war upon the seceding Southern States was based upon two major points he announced in his March 1861 inaugural address and his July 4, 1861 message to Congress. It is important to remember that the death of almost one million Americans, soldiers and civilians, and the intentional impoverishment of the formerly prosperous South was based upon Lincoln and the Republican Party's allegation that: (1) The States of the Union were never sovereign and therefore sovereignty resides with the Federal government; (2) the Union is older than the Constitution and the Union created the States, and therefore was older than the States.

If sovereignty resides with the Union, i.e., the Federal government, then secession is illegal and tantamount to treason. But if sovereignty resides with "we the people" of each sovereign State, then secession is legal and the natural and logical pursuit of the American principle of "government by the consent of the governed." The political upheaval caused by the Chisolm case demonstrates that Americans believed that the right of self-government, consent of the governed, and other attributes of sovereignty resided with "we the people" within their respective states. Alexander Hamilton in *The Federalist* No. 81, proclaimed, "It is inherent in the nature of sovereignty, not to be amenable to the suit of an individual without its consent...as one of the attributes of sovereignty, is now enjoyed by the government of every state in the union."[11] The uproar caused by the Supreme Court's attack upon State sovereignty in 1793 crossed all geographic lines. The day after the *Chisolm v. Georgia* decision was announced, Massachusetts Representative Theodore Sedgwick introduced a resolution to amend the Constitution. His proposed amendment would prevent a sovereign state from being compelled against its will to appear before a Federal Court.

---

11   Alexander Hamilton, as cited in, Carey and McClellan, *The Federalist* (Dubuque, IA: Kendall/Hunt Publishing co., 1990), 420-21.

On the floor of the House of Representatives, Rep. Sedgwick stated: "Mr. Speaker. But yesterday a majority decision of a most alarming nature was handed down by the Supreme Court. Sir, I rise to protest in the name of Massachusetts against this decision. It gives a new and wrong construction of the character of this Government. It reduces free and independent sovereignties to the rank of mere provinces. It contradicts the Declaration of Independence, which solemnly declares, 'That these united Colonies are, and of right ought to be, free and independent States.' Nor can the United States lawfully rob them of their rights as sovereign States until the Tenth Amendment...is repealed."[12] Sedgwick's resolution passed In the House of Representatives by a vote of 81 yes and 9 no votes (90%). In the Senate this resolution passed by 23 yes and 2 no votes (92%). For a Constitutional Amendment to pass Congress and be submitted to the States requires a 2/3s or 66% affirmative vote of both houses. As demonstrated, the Eleventh Amendment greatly surpassed that threshold. When submitted to the States, there being fifteen States in the Union at that time, thirteen States voted for the Amendment with no dissenting votes. "This amendment was designed to silence forever all doubts as to the sovereignty of the States."[13] Unfortunately for America, Lincoln and the Republicans were either ignorant of this history or willfully ignored this bold announcement of State sovereignty.

What then was Lincoln's "enlightened" view of State or Federal sovereignty? Let us look at Lincoln's own words as it relates to State and Federal sovereignty. In his July 4, 1861 address to Congress, Lincoln boldly proclaimed, "Much is said about the 'sovereignty' of the states, but the word even is not in the National Constitution, nor, as is believed, in any of the State constitutions." Lincoln declares that since the word "sovereignty" cannot be found in the National Constitution, no State can be sovereign. Keeping with Lincoln's logic, we are compelled to ask: "Since the National Constitution of the United States does not have the word "sovereignty" in it, does this mean that the United States is not a sovereign nation?"

---

12   Theodore Sedgwick, as cited in, J. A. Richardson, *A Historical and Constitutional Defense of The South* (1914, Harrisonburg, VA: Sprinkle Publication, 2010), 266-67.

13   J. A. Richardson, *Ibid.,* 267.

Lincoln's own words demonstrates his sophomoric understanding of the Constitution! The Constitution is not a cookbook of rights that the Federal government grants to Americans. The Constitution is a document from "we the people" of the States that delegates power from each State in order to create a Federal government and therefore, the Union. As is noted in the Tenth Amendment, "The powers not delegated... are reserved to the States respectively, or to the people." Also, as noted in the Ninth Amendment, "The enumeration...of certain rights, shall not be construed to deny or disparage others retained by the people." These two amendments speak with an honest and forceful voice that just because something is not in the Constitution that does not mean that "we the people" do not hold that right or power. For example, the word "marriage" does not occur in the Constitution but as we fully understand, Americans have the right to marry.

The positive response of the vast majority of Americans by ratifying the Eleventh Amendment in response to the Supreme Court's Chisolm decision, proves that Americans were aggressively defending the principle of State sovereignty. Sixty-three years after the adoption of the Eleventh Amendment, Lincoln would declare that no State was ever sovereign. Upon that false premise Lincoln and the Republican Party would instigate America's most bloody war—a genocidal war of conquest. If these facts surrounding the adoption of the Eleventh Amendment were the only evidence of State sovereignty, that alone would be enough to condemn Lincoln and the Republican Party as rabid war-criminals. But there is more, much more.

As previously noted, Lincoln asserted that the Union was older than the States and "the Union created the States." This "fact" would have come as a great surprise to the people of each colony as they and they alone expelled all Royal (English) authority from their colony and assumed full control of their colony. From 1609, the founding of Jamestown, Virginia, to 1774, the first meeting of the Continental Congress (165 yrs.) there was no union, government, or official association among the Thirteen North American Colonies. The only union that existed was the union between each separate colony and Great Britain.

Many nationalist scholars have proclaimed the First Continental Congress (1774) to be the first government of what was to become the United States. What these so-call scholars selectively choose to ignore is that the Continental Congress had no power to command nor enforce any of its resolutions. The Continental Congress was strictly a deliberative body that could recommend anything but conclude nothing! It was more akin to a social club than to a government. As Bodin pointed out, a sovereign has the power to command,[14] the Continental Congress did not command, it recommended. The only government in America at that time which could command and enforce its command were the individual sovereign States of America. In reference to the Continental Congress, Judge Able Upshur noted, "that body was not a general or national government, nor a government of any kind... its acts were not in the form of laws but recommendation...it could command nothing."[15] Each colony elected delegates to the Continental Congress but each colony had only one vote regardless of size or population, again pointing to the sovereign nature of each colony. Throwing off all Royal authority, appointing delegates to the Continental Congress, and empowering said delegates to vote for or against independence, was being performed by "we the people" of each sovereign State without the aid or assistance of Mr. Lincoln's mystical Union.

In 1775 the Continental Congress recommended that Continental Officers should take the following oath, "I do acknowledge that the Thirteen United States of America, namely [each individual State was then named] to be free independent and sovereign states... ." Is it not shocking to note that Abraham Lincoln's view of sovereign States runs counter to the oath taken by the brave men in 1775 who were fighting for America's Rights? On July 4, 1776 the delegates who voted for independence did not do so upon their own desire but could only vote for or against independence if given that authority by their State. Throughout the Declaration of Independence when speaking of the Colonies or States, the plural noun or pronoun is used, whereas when speaking of Great Britain, the singular noun or

---

14 Jean Bodin, *Op. Cit. 3*.

15 Able Upshur, *The Federal Government: Its True Nature and Character* (New York: Van Evrie, Horton, & Co., 1868), 50.

pronoun is used. If these United States were "one nation indivisible" and under the guidance of Lincoln's omnipotent and mystical Union, why speak of States in the plural? In 1783 the Treaty of Paris was signed in which King George recognized the independence of these United States. The treaty states, "His Britannic Majesty acknowledges the said United States, viz, [at this point he names each of the thirteen States] to be free sovereign and independent States, that he treats with them as such..." [16] After the recognition of United States independence, the first real government, and therefore first Union, was established under the Articles of Confederation. Article II of said Articles clearly states, "Each state retains its sovereignty, freedom, and independence and every Power and Jurisdiction and right, which is not by this confederation expressly delegated to the United States." So once again it is clearly noted in the record of these United States that, regardless of Mr. Lincoln's fake history, real history proves that the States were and are sovereign. A common way to write the name of the country in the early republic was the "united States," as state sovereignty was a given. As explained in the Declaration of Independence, the people of each State had the American right to live in a government by the "consent of the governed" and to "alter or abolish it [government], and institute new Government" at their will.

Secession is the means by which the abolishing of bad government and the establishment of "new Government" is accomplished. Lincoln, the sixteenth president, said that since the States are not sovereign, attempting secession was an act of rebellion. Lincoln is only one president, what was the view of previous presidents on the issue of secession? Is Lincoln's view the only American view about secession?

During the War of 1812, a very unpopular war in New England, several New England States began discussing the need to secede from the Union. Thomas Jefferson's response to the news of New Englanders seeking the option of secession (1813-14) is very different from Lincoln's reaction in 1861. When faced with the possibility of some New England States seeking secession, Jefferson wrote that they should "call a convention of their State, and to require them to declare themselves members of the Union...

---

16 Treaty of Paris 1783, Paris Peace Treaty Text (varsitytutors.com) Accessed 2/7/21.

or not members, and let them go. Put this question solemnly to their people, and their answer cannot be doubtful."[17] Here Jefferson is recurring to the idea that the American people, via their sovereign State, have the right to "alter or abolish" their government. He rejects the idea of coercion or war to force people back into a union in which the people feel that they are being oppressed. If forced back into such a union Jefferson warns that, "near friends falling out, never reunite cordially."[18] Lincoln's use of force to "save the Union" is opposite from Jefferson's view of the Union.

Jefferson, a Southerner, was joined in 1830 by the sixth president of the United States, John Q. Adams of Massachusetts, in advocating peaceful secession rather than the use of coercion and war to "save the Union." The Union of States united by a "fraternal spirit" was so important to President John Q. Adams, that he advocated peaceful secession rather than war to keep states in a union of discontented members. Adams said, "If the day should ever come...when the affections of the people of the states shall be alienated from each other; when fraternal spirit shall give away to cold indifference... far better it be for the people of the disunited states, to part in friendship from each other, THAN TO BE HELD TOGETHER BY CONSTRAINT"[19] [emphasis added]. Lincoln did not get that memo!

The belief in State sovereignty was so strong that when William Rawle of Philadelphia, Pennsylvania wrote his textbook on the Constitution (1825), he included a chapter on how and why a State could secede from the Union. Rawle's textbook was reviewed by the well-respected journal 'The North American Review' of Boston, Massachusetts, without one negative comment on Rawle's view of the right of secession.[20] Only 36 years after these Boston intellectuals gave a glowing review of Rawle's textbook, they joined Lincoln and

---

17 Thomas Jefferson, as cited in, William B. Parker and Jonas Viles, eds., *Letters and Addresses of Thomas Jefferson* (Buffalo, NY: National Jefferson Society, 1903), 231.

18 *Ibid.*, 68.

19 John Q. Adams, cited in Joshua Horne, "John Quincy Adams on Secession," *Discerning History*, 27 July 2013, (tinyurl.com/yywbqmok) Accessed 7/4/2020.

20 *North American Review* (1826, NY: AMs Press, Inc., 1965), XXII, 446-51.

the Republican Party by insisting that the States were not sovereign and therefore, could not secede.

Other presidents also acknowledged the sovereignty of the States. John Tyler, the 10th president, became a member of the Confederate States Congress and defended the rights of the States against Lincoln's aggression. Franklin Pierce, of New Hampshire, the 14th president, was a strong States' Rights man and close friend of Jefferson Davis. Pierce feared the concentration of power into a strong Federal government. Pierce stated, "The dangers of a concentration of all power in the general government...so vast as ours are too obvious to be disregarded... . The great scheme of our constitutional liberty rests upon a proper distribution of power between the State and Federal authorities."[21] During the debates over adopting the Constitution two of America's most influential found fathers, James Madison (4th president) and Alexander Hamilton wrote in *The Federalist* that the States were indeed, sovereign States. Madison in *The Federalist* No. 39 clearly notes, "Each State in ratifying the Constitution, is considered as a sovereign body independent of all others, and only to be bound by its own voluntary act." Hamilton in *The Federalists* No. 85 declares the States to be, "thirteen independent states." These free, independent, and therefore sovereign States have the American Right to "alter or abolish" their government at their will. Note that Madison in *The Federalists* No. 39 declares that each State is "bound by its own voluntary act." How much more proof is needed to establish that the States are sovereign and therefore have the right to withdraw its consent, i.e., secede, from any government?

These five presidents who preceded Lincoln (Jefferson, Madison, Pierce, Adams, and Tyler) dispute Lincoln's idea of Federal sovereignty and the Right of the Federal government to use force to "save the Union." If the Union cannot be maintained by force, how is it to be maintained? James Kent of New York answers that question for all Americans. Kent stated, "On the concurrence and good will of the parts [States], the stability of the whole [Union] depends."[22]

---

21 Franklin Pierce Inaugural Address, March 1853, as cited in Franklin Pierce: Inaugural Address. U.S. Inaugural Addresses. 1989 (bartleby.com) Accessed 2-8-21.

22 James Kent, *Commentaries on American Law* (1826, NY: Da Capo Press, 1871), I, 594.

An immensely important question that most Americans refuse to consider is, "What type of union was "saved" by Lincoln and the Republican Party's use of bloody bayonets?" A reading of *The Federalists* and other documents relating to the adoption of the Constitution provides abundant evidence that the Union "saved" by being forcefully "reunited," is NOT the original Union established by America's Founding Fathers. Once the Federal government began treating sovereign States as conquered provinces, where rights and freedom are permitted or denied by an all-powerful and indivisible Union, the old Union died. Comparing the old Union of sovereign States, who in 1798 demanded that the Federal government recognize the sovereign nature of the States in passing the Eleventh Amendment, to the supreme, all-powerful, indivisible new Union of today reveals a sad truth. The sad truth is that the new Union, created by Lincoln and the Republican Party, has more in common with the Union of Soviet Socialists Republic (a supreme, all-powerful, and indivisible union) than the old Union composed of many sovereign States. The Soviet Union, like all empires, used force or the threat of force to keep conquered States within their Union—no different than Mr. Lincoln.

Is it any wonder that Communist China has repeatedly stated that when it determines to use force to regain control of Taiwan, it will only be following the lead of Lincoln and the Republican Party? The policy of Communist China using force to retake Taiwan was reported in an article in the 'Bloomberg News' titled 'China Invokes Abraham Lincoln in Justifying Push to Take Taiwan.'[23] This headline alone should give every American who loves liberty and freedom a reason to reconsider Lincoln and the Republican Party's invasion and conquest of the Confederate States of America.

A year after the defeat of the South, General Lee, in a letter to Lord Acton of Great Britain, warned that with the death of real States' Rights, the United States would become "aggressive abroad and despotic at home." Today, the United States has embraced General Lee's prophetic warning. The only way to rein in this imperial, overgrown behemoth of an all-powerful, big government is to force the Federal government to recognize the sovereign nature of "we

---

23 "China Invokes Abraham Lincoln in Justifying Push to Take Taiwan," Bloomberg News, June 1, 2019.

the people" of each State. Standard business-as-usual politics will not get this job done. Recent history proves that standard politics, that is, electing more conservatives, putting more "good" judges on the Supreme Court, or electing a good man as president, cannot control the Deep State behemoth. The fraudulent election of 2020 demonstrates that our enemies are too strong and entrenched to be defeated by using an election process controlled by Deep State operatives. We must develop a new and different method of political action in order to regain control of our Federal government. We must use our strength against their weakness—the very opposite of what "conservatives" have been doing for the past one hundred years. A new generation of conservatives must learn how to use asymmetrical, i.e., irregular political warfare to regain our Rights.

A good starting point for asymmetrical political warfare would be to organize something like the Tea Party, but this time, we must organize a Tea Party with TEETH! This new effort must be responsible for forming provisional governments in each State that will act as a lobbying group from the local level to the State legislature. Not only will provisional governments lobby for real change but it must work locally to inform the public of the need to defeat RINOs and as the state's Provisional government gets stronger, elect our people. The one main focus of these provisional governments is to push for our State Sovereignty Constitutional Amendment. This amendment will force the Federal government to recognize each State as sovereign and fully capable of exercising the rights of nullification and/or secession. The text of this Amendment can be found at www.kennedytwins.com, the Kennedy Twins website.[24] For a more complete description of irregular political warfare, read *Dixie Rising: Rules for Rebels*, 2nd edition.[25] A quick review of *Dixie Rising*, will demonstrate that this effort is something never tried before and has great potential to, like the 1793 *Chisholm v Georgia* decision, "set the nation in an uproar."

Just ten years after the adoption of the Constitution by the "separate and independent" action of "we the people" of sovereign States, the Eleventh Amendment underscored and re-proclaimed

---

24 bit.ly/sovereignty-ammendment

25 James R. Kennedy, *Dixie Rising: Rules for Rebels,* 2nd edition (Columbia, SC: Shotwell Publishing, 2021).

that these United States were a republic of sovereign States. As sovereign States they had the power to over-rule any Federal abuse and if necessary, recall their delegated power. In *The Federalist* No. 43, James Madison notes why secession or recalling delegated rights is necessary, "the safety and happiness of society are the objects at which all political institutions must be sacrificed." The "Union" falls within Madison's definition of "all political institutions." While debating the adoption of the Constitution, Patrick Henry informs Americans which "institution," government or liberty, is most important when he said, "The first thing I have at heart is American liberty, the second thing is American union." These founding fathers and the patriots who ratified the Eleventh Amendment, understood that in a free society liberty always trumps government. Bold action today can re-establish that type of government for our children's and grandchildren's future.

Chapter XXIII

THE LITTLE VERB THAT CAUSED A BIG WAR

THE 2020 PRESIDENTIAL ELECTION controversy has given rise to many questions about the Electoral College and why Americans elect their President by such a non-democratic system. Most Americans are shocked to learn that if the Electoral College cannot elect a president, the House of Representatives, voting by state with each state having only ONE vote, would determine the president. In both cases, the election is very un-democratic. Many have asked, why does Wyoming with only 578,000 population have the same number of votes for president in the House of Representatives as California with almost 40 million population? In both cases the answer is embarrassing to conservative and liberal political pundits. This fact is also shocking to the average American. The answer that shocks people is that this system of presidential election is done because American States were once sovereign. States' Rights exist because States, prior to 1865, were sovereign. The loss of State Sovereignty was lamented by Confederate General Bradley Johnson of Maryland: "The time will come when all the world will realize that the failure of the Confederacy was...the source of unnumbered woes to liberty."[26]

Ken Burns 1990 "Civil War" series became a blockbuster soon after its release. Early in the series Burn observed that the War was fought over whether the verb "is" or the verb "are" would be used to describe the United States of America. For example, which is correct: The United States "is" a republic or the United States "are" a republic? The answer to that question was fundamental to the cause of the 1861 conflict. If these United States "is" a republic,

---

26 Bradley T. Johnson, *Southern Historical Papers,* XXIII, 368.

sovereignty resides with a SINGLE entity, the Federal government. Yet, if the United States "are" a republic, sovereignty belongs to EACH sovereign state, NOT the Federal government. More simply stated, is the United States a "one nation indivisible" republic or is the United States a republic of sovereign States or as Madison describes the United States, "a compound republic"? If the United States is a republic composed of federated republics, then each republic, that is, each state, is sovereign and has the right to judge for itself how it is to be governed. Yes, the Federal government exercises certain powers of sovereignty but those powers are derived from authority delegated to it from the states. In other words, the states exercise original sovereignty while the federal government exercises only secondary sovereignty.

As the Burns' series quickly demonstrated, he was acting as an agent of the victorious North by defending the idea of Federal sovereignty. The Federal supremacy theory of the U.S.A. being "one nation indivisible" was promoted throughout the series. Burns dismisses any evidence that the United States was ever anything but "one nation indivisible," so therefore, "is" was the correct verb to use in identifying the United States. Throughout his series the history of the War and events leading up to the War were told in such a manner as to leave the viewer with the impression that the North was virtuous and correct while the South was immoral and wrong. But Burns was correct when he noted that the War centered around the use of a verb. His observation was correct but, as historical evidence demonstrates, his conclusion was totally incorrect.

As many Southerners have proclaimed, the War was fought for States' Rights. But where does States' Rights originate and what ultimately defines a Right of a State? States' Rights flows from the principle of state sovereignty. A sovereign state has rights that are particular to a sovereign entity. Within the boundary of a sovereign state, only those rules that are agreed upon by the state can operate. Within the American system of government, the most fundamental Right of "we the people" of a sovereign state is the Right to live in a government by the "consent of the governed." This is plainly acknowledged in the Declaration of Independence when it announces that the people have the unalienable Right and obligation to "alter or abolish" any government they do not like and to establish a new government more to their liking. The Declaration of Independence also proclaims that the only LEGITIMATE government is one based upon the "consent of the governed."

To understand why traditional Southerners believe that the South was right, we must understand the foundation for the American principle of States' Rights. To defend the South's right of secession and independence, we must recognize the location and nature of sovereignty in these United States. Burns promotes Lincoln's myth about the location and nature of sovereignty in the United States. Lincoln stated that no state was or had ever been sovereign and that sovereignty ultimately belonged to the Federal government—the United States "IS". Lincoln's view was not new in American history but up until 1865, it was a minority view of American government. The antecedents of Lincoln's view reach back to the early hyper-Federalists. Hyper-Federalists sought to impose upon the newly independent nation a supreme indivisible federal government—a Federal government that was answerable only to itself. At every turn the hyper-Federalists were met by men such as Jefferson, Madison, Calhoun, and the vast majority of American patriots (North and South) and defeated. But like all radicals, even when suffering a tactical defeat, they never gave up on making this nation an "IS" (one nation indivisible) nation rather than an "ARE" (a republic of republics) nation.

Politically, the hyper-Federalists found a home in the Federalists Party which morphed into the Whig Party, which later became part of the Republican Party. All three parties desired to increase the power of the Federal government and use that power to promote the well-being of those close to the political establishment. Thus, we see the march toward a big one nation indivisible Federal government, the grandparent of today's Deep State. The drive to convert the original United States from a compound republic, i.e., a republic of republics, although stymied at times, continued until the Republican victory in 1860. As shall be demonstrated, with Lincoln's election and the sad defeat of the Confederate States of America, REAL States' Rights died. Even General Lee, a rather non-political military leader, admitted that with the defeat of the South, America, like any empire, would become "aggressive abroad and despotic at home."

Lincoln and the Republican Party marched to victory by advocating two false and deadly ideas about the nature of the Federal government: (1) The states of the Union were never sovereign, and (2) the Union existed before the states and created the states. In his July 1861 message to Congress, Lincoln stated that no state was or had ever been sovereign. So, following the false logic of Lincoln and the Republicans, a state cannot be sovereign and therefore does not possess the Right of self-government, i.e., government by the consent of the governed. In his July 1861 message to Congress, Lincoln proclaimed, "Much is said about the 'sovereignty' of the states, but the word even is not in the National Constitution, nor, as is believed, in any of the State constitutions."[27] According to Lincoln and the Republican Party, sovereignty is vested only in the Federal government. This "logic" denies to "we the people" of the states the right to judge how we are to be governed, only the Federal government is vested with that power.

Let's test Lincoln's assertion that since the word sovereignty does not exist in the Constitution, no state can be sovereign and that the word sovereignty does not exist in any state constitution. Lincoln is correct, the word "sovereignty" cannot be found in the Constitution but does that mean states are not sovereign? The same "logic" can also be applied to the Federal government. If the word sovereignty does not exist within the FEDERAL Constitution does that mean that the FEDERAL government is not sovereign? Lincoln's logic leaves us with something that cannot exist; an un-sovereign nation. To further demonstrate the absurdity of Lincoln's statement, let us ask: Can the word "marriage" be found in the Constitution, and if not, does that mean that there are no legal marriages in the United States? Let the Constitution speak for itself. Any power, authority, or right that is NOT delegated to the Federal government, such as, marriage, nullification, owning property, or secession, remain with the people or the States. The words of the Ninth and Tenth Amendments destroys Lincoln's false logic.

It should be noted that the Ninth Amendment clearly states, "The enumeration in the Constitution of certain rights, shall not be construed to deny or disparage others retained by the people."

---

27 Abraham Lincoln, "July 4th Message to Congress," 4 July 1861.

When Lincoln denied that "we the people" of the states have the right to "alter or abolish" the government we lived under, he was "disparaging" retained rights of the people. As the Tenth Amendment proclaims, that which is not denied to the states or delegated to the Federal government, "are reserved to the states respectively, or to the people." Lincoln has turned the Constitution into a cookbook of rights that the Federal government allows Americans to exercise and the Federal government becomes the sole judge of how and when we exercise those rights—what tyrant could ask for more power?

In his message to Congress, Lincoln stated that no state had ever been sovereign and even the word sovereign cannot be found in any state constitution. Even more absurd is Lincoln's claim that, "The Union is older than the States and in fact created them as States...and made them States, such as they are."[28] Two examples will disprove Lincoln's incorrect claim that the word "sovereignty" did not exist in any state constitution. The State of New Hampshire's Constitution proclaims, "The people of this Commonwealth have the sole and exclusive right of governing themselves as a free, sovereign, and independent State... ."[29] The State of Louisiana's first Constitution clearly stated that it entered the Union as "a free and independent State."[30] A sovereign state is a free and independent state and a free and independent state is a sovereign state. The attributes of sovereignty were clearly held by the people of each state as they entered the new Union.

Even Alexander Hamilton, a hyper-Federalists, acknowledged the states as independent states. In *'The Federalists'* Hamilton states the United States consists of "thirteen independent states... ."[31] Hamilton goes further by asserting that these "independent states" would be capable to "erect barriers against the encroachments of

---

28 Ibid.

29 New Hampshire Constitution as cited in, *The American's Guide to the Constitution of the United States of America* (Trenton: Moore and Lake, 1813) 341.

30 Ibid.

31 Alexander Hamilton *The Federalist* No. 85 as cited in George W. Carey and James McClellan, (Dubuque, IA: Kendall/Hunt Publishing, 1990), 452.

the national authority."[32] Madison in *The Federalists* notes that the Constitution would be ratified "by the people, not as individuals composing one entire nation [not one nation indivisible]; but as composing the distinct and independent States...Each State...is considered as a sovereign body independent of all others and only bound by its own voluntary act."[33] Madison makes it clear that no constitution, union, or government should be maintained unless it protected the "safety and happiness" of the people. Madison clearly proclaims that, "the safety and happiness of society are the objects at which all political institutions must be sacrificed."[34] More dramatic is his declaration that if the Union was "adverse to public happiness, my voice would be...abolish the Union."[35] Two of our Founding Fathers, Hamilton and Madison, are describing a Union that Lincoln and the Republican Party refused to acknowledge—a voluntary Union of sovereign State united for their MUTUAL benefit.

The Union of States united by a "fraternal spirit" was so important to President John Q. Adams of Massachusetts, that he advocated peaceful secession rather than war to keep states in a union of discontented members. Adams said, "If the day should ever come...when the affections of the people of the states shall be alienated from each other; when fraternal spirit shall give away to cold indifference...far better it be for the people of the disunited states, to part in friendship from each other, THAN TO BE HELD TOGETHER BY CONSTRAINT"[36] [emphasis added]. Lincoln did not get that memo!

Most Americans understand that the Declaration of Independence announced American independence from Great Britain. Yet few understand how the delegates who voted for independence were selected. In a council of sovereign states, such as, NATO, UN, or any other international organization, each state, regardless of size, wealth,

---

32 Ibid., 453.

33 James Madison, 'The Federalist No. 39,' Ibid., 197.

34 Ibid., 'The Federalist No. 43,' 228.

35 Ibid., 'The Federalist No. 45,' 235-36.

36 John Q. Adams, cited in Joshua Horne, "John Quincy Adams on Secession," Discerning History, 27 July 2013, (tinyurl.com/yywbqmok) Accessed 7/4/2020.

or population, is considered as an equal and allowed one vote at council meetings. When the thirteen colonies took control of their own colonial governments, each colony became a sovereign state. Therefore, when sending delegates to the Continental Congress each state, regardless of size, wealth, or population, had one vote in Congress. A state could send any number of delegates but the delegates had only one vote for their state—no different than the vote for president in the House of Representatives. When voting for independence, the delegation from each state had to consult with or have permission from their state legislature to vote for or against independence—they were bound by their state. These actions of the state prove that each state was sovereign well before the Union was created and that the states were sovereign well before July 4, 1776 (remember that Lincoln said that the Union existed BEFORE the states).

According to the Journal of the Continental Congress, on October 29, 1776 it was recommended that all officers of the Continental military take the following oath: "I do acknowledge that the Thirteen United States of America, namely [each State is then named] to be free independent and sovereign states... ."[37] The oath continues disavowing any allegiance to King George or any of his heirs. It seems very obvious that the members of the Continental Congress correctly understood that the States existed and were sovereign States. Yet, Lincoln and the Republican Party maintain these Colonial Delegates were incorrect. Lincoln then waged a genocidal war against thirteen sovereign states to "prove" that he and the Republican Party were right.

The very words of both the Declaration of Independence (1776) and the Treaty of Paris (1783) informs the world that each of the thirteen states of America were "free and independent" states. Once again it must be pointed out that a "free and independent" state is a sovereign state. Here is a summary of evidence that proves Lincoln and the Republican Party were incorrect in stating that the Union preceded the states and actually created the states: (1) the individual states elected and empowered their delegates to represent them in the Continental Congress; (2) each state empowered said delegates to vote for or against independence; (3) each state determined

---

37 *Journal of the Continental Congress, 10/9/1776*, Library of Congress, VI, 893-94.

for itself whether to join the first Union under the Articles of Confederation; (4) each state determined for itself to secede from the Union under the Articles of Confederation and join (accede) the new Union under the Constitution; (5) the Continental Congress proposed that all officers of the military take an oath recognizing the independence and sovereignty of the States and, (6) Article VII of the Constitution clearly and unequivocally proclaims that the states, acting independent from each other, would determine if they were to join the new Union under the Constitution. When reviewing this evidence, it becomes abundantly clear that Lincoln and the Republican Party were woefully incorrect in asserting that these United States "is" rather than "are" a republic.

Although most prominent conservative commentators embrace Lincoln as an advocate of small government, they completely overlook the fact that two of the world's most notorious big government advocates were admirers of Lincoln. In Mein Kampf, Adolph Hitler follows Lincoln's "logic" about the Union creating the states of the United States. Hitler noted, "The states that make up the American Union are mostly in the natures of territories. These states did not and could not possess sovereign rights of their own. Because it was the Union that created most of these so-called states."[38] Notice that Hitler agrees with Lincoln on two very important points, the states were not sovereign and the Union created (therefore existed before) "these so-called states." Where Hitler refers to American States as "so called states," Lincoln refers to these States as "such as they are." Before Hitler glowingly reported upon the work of Lincoln and the Republican Party in making the United States "one nation indivisible," Karl Marx was already praising Lincoln. In an address written by Marx congratulating Lincoln on his second presidential victory, Marx anointed Lincoln as, "the single-minded son of the working class, to lead his country through the matchless struggle for...the reconstruction of a social world."[39] History proves that freedom is destroyed in every nation that has undergone

---

38 Adolf Hitler, *Mein Kampf* (New York: Hurst and Blackett, LTD, 1942), 312.

39 Karl Marx, "Address of the International Workingmen's Association to Abraham Lincoln," as cited in Marx and Engels, *Letters to Americans,* (New York: International Publishers Co., Inc., 1953), 72.

communist "reconstruction of a social world." This "reconstruction" always ushers in rank poverty and death—not unlike what the South suffered after its conquest and "reconstruction."

Fredrick Engels, co-author along with Marx of the Communist Manifesto, sheds light upon why those who love big government hate States' Rights and push the narrative of "one nation indivisible." In a letter to his friend and fellow communist, Union General Weydemeyer, Engels praised the North's effort to defeat the South because as he notes, the war would tend to promote, "The preliminaries of the proletarian revolution, the measures that prepare the battleground and clear the way for us, such as a single and indivisible republic."[40] In another place Engels announces that the successful defeat of the South would "doubtless determine the future of America for hundreds of years to come."[41]

With the defeat of the South in 1865, the proponents of "one nation indivisible" destroyed the Union given to America by her Founding Fathers and imposed upon all Americans a union of which men such as Marx, Engels, and Hitler could and did admire. Is it any wonder that today no American State can effectively resist the power of the supreme "one nation indivisible" Federal government? Federal sovereignty equals Federal domination, whereas State sovereignty equals local control of government via real States' Rights.

After the War in an address in honor of Lincoln, Col. Robert G. Ingersoll of the Eleventh Illinois Cavalry, a Freethinker, a Radical Abolitionist, and Republican, noted, "The great stumbling block, the great obstruction in Lincoln's way AND IN THE WAY OF THOUSANDS, was the old doctrine of States' Rights."[42] Yes, States' Rights did stand in the way of thousands of those who would misuse the power of government to create a utopian, socialist big government. Without REAL States' Rights, an all-powerful government that is answerable only to itself was not only possible, it was inevitable!

---

40 Fredrick Engels, *Ibid.*, 57.

41 *Ibid.*, 63.

42 Robert G. Ingersoll, "Abraham Lincoln, a lecture," Speech given 1894 as cited in (http://www.archive.org/stream/abrahamlincolnle00inge/abrahamlincolnle00inge_djvu.txt) Accessed March 16, 2009.

This is why men such as Thomas Jefferson, James Madison, St. George Tucker, William Rawle and John Q. Adams, among thousands of others, believed in the right of secession. The ever-present threat of secession forces the Federal government to live and act within the limits of the Constitution, otherwise, responding to an abusive Federal government, secession would ensue. Without this option, all that is left for "we the people" of the once sovereign states to do is to prostrate ourselves before the might of an all-powerful, one nation indivisible, Federal tyranny.

While praising the Federal victory over the South, the co-founder of modern communism, Fredrick Engels, correctly noted that the Federal victory would, "doubtless determine the future of America for hundreds of years to come." That victory was a victory for a big, one nation indivisible, supreme Federal government filled with Deep State operatives. Until Americans regain the Constitutional rights lost at Appomattox, that is, REAL States' Rights, General Lee's prediction of an "aggressive abroad and despotic at home" Federal government will remain the lot of all Americans. Today more than anytime in this author's life, non-Southerners are beginning to understand what Confederate Vice President Alexander Stephens meant when he said, "The only hope for its [Constitutional Liberty] preservation... on this Continent, is, that a cry be raised... from Atlantic to the Pacific: The Cause of the South is the Cause of us all!"[43] The Constitution is not self-enforcing. Without the ability to use the States' Rights of nullification and/or secession, the Constitution is nothing but a paper barricade behind which our liberties cannot survive. Americans in general and Southerners in particular would be well served to consider ways to restore Constitutional liberty via REAL States' Rights before even more drastic action is called upon.

DEO VINDICE!

---

43 Alexander H. Stephens, *A Constitutional View of the late War Between the States*, (Harrisonburg, VA: Sprinkle Publications, 1994), II, 666.

CONCLUDING COMMENTS

AMERICA'S HOPE:
ANOTHER TIME AND ANOTHER FORM

From the introduction of this work to the final chapter, three themes have been stressed: (1) The efforts of defending and promoting the truth about Southern history and culture have not been successful, (2) a new approach must be found to not just push back the enemies of the South but to defeat, crush, and annihilate those who hate not just Southern history but the people of the South, and (3) it is not just the South that neo-Marxists seek to destroy. Neo-Marxists seek the ultimate and complete destruction of all Traditional American Values. As is demonstrated in chapters XXII and XXIII, true Southern history destroys the false claims of the neo-Marxist rabble. These chapters along with a vast collection of books, articles, and videos by well-established historians and commentators prove that we have all the facts needed to win any fair debate. Our problem is not a deficiency of facts but a lack of a robust means of getting that information to John Q. Public.

Recent polling across the South on the issue of removing Confederate monuments and memorials found that 60% to 75% of Southerners were in favor of maintaining Confederate monuments. A nationwide poll of non-Southern States demonstrated that from 45% to 54% of Americans were against the removal of Confederate monuments and memorials. Clearly, we have the majority of Americans in general and Southerners in particular on our side. Why then are we seeing one monument after another being removed? Why is there not an end to the never-ceasing cultural cleansing of the South? Have you ever heard the old truism, "The squeaky wheel gets the grease"? Our enemies are organized both for public demonstrations and political action—they are America's squeaky wheel. The Southern Movement is not organized for anything more than holding heady Civil War lecture series, cleaning cemeteries, ancestor research, filing lawsuits in a judicial system controlled by the anti-South establishment, and promoting "Civil War" re-enactments. None of these efforts are wrong or useless—except if this is all that we do. We Southerners have been doing these things for the past fifty years; we were losing then and we are still losing! Maybe it's time to rethink both our strategy and our tactics.

One of the most important lessons any military leader must learn is to never give your enemy the battle he desires to fight. If your enemy has the best and most numerous battle tanks, you must not allow him to draw you into a live-or-die tank battle. A good military leader knows how to use his strength against his enemies' weakness. Understanding this concept is basic to planning and executing any victorious battle plan.

At this point in time, the South's greatest strength resides in the fact that 60% to 75% of Southerners still love the South's heritage. This gives those of us who are fighting to preserve our heritage and defeat our enemies, the "homefield advantage." This also points out the weakness of our enemies. The job of Southern patriots should be centered around educating the Southern populace about the glory of our Southland, motivating Southerners to speak up in defense of our Southland, and activating a large portion of the educated and motivated populace to become actively involved (as members of various Southern Rights organizations) in pushing for total victory over the enemies of Traditional American Values, which of course, includes Southern heritage/history.

As Ron points out in chapter XXI there is a path to total victory but we must embrace new ideas about how to fight this battle. Strategically, the ultimate goal of the Southern movement is to reform or replace the current illegitimate Federal government. Lincoln's illegitimate government must be replaced with a Constitutionally legitimate Federal government as given us by our Founding Fathers. This is why the push for the Sovereign State Amendment is so important. This Amendment returns to "we the people" our rightful place as the final judge of the actions of the Federal government.

Just as important is exactly which tactics should be used to promote our effort for final victory. As demonstrated by the left-wing orchestrated, January 6, 2021 so-called "insurrection," the enemy will use any method to destroy their opponents. Yes, the left has been very successful using mass demonstrations and violence to promote their cause. That does not mean that we can duplicate their methods. Remember, the left has the political establishment, media, and academia constantly running interference for them. If our side attempted such action, the full force of the government would come down hard on us. If we tried to "surround our monuments with our guns" in an effort to protect them, do you really think the government would simply back down and leave us alone? To act in such a manner is tantamount to giving the enemy the battle he wants to fight—that is not how you fight smart!

We can win this battle and put an end to the cultural cleansing of the South and of all Traditional American Values if we learn how to fight smart. We must give our enemies the battle they cannot win and we will be victorious. Go back and re-read chapter XXI. Get a copy of *Dixie Rising: Rules for Rebels,* and let's start fighting smart. By committing yourself to making THIS DAY that "another time and another form," we will fulfill the Charge given to the South by General Stephen D. Lee. At that time, we will "vindicate the Cause for which they fought" and thereby secure real American liberty and freedom for future generations of Americans. Deo Vindice.

> The principle for which we contended is bound to reassert itself, though it may be at <u>another time</u> and in <u>another form</u>.
>
> —President Jefferson Davis, CSA

ABOUT THE AUTHOR

Walter Donald (Donnie) Kennedy was born and reared in Mississippi with his twin brother James Ronald (Ron) Kennedy. Each received his Bachelor's degree from the University of Louisiana, Monroe, Louisiana. Donnie is also a graduate of Charlotte Memorial Medical Center School of Anesthesia, Charlotte, North Carolina.

The Kennedy Twins are best known for their bestselling book *The South Was Right!*, which has sold over 135,000 copies. Following the success of *The South Was Right!*, the Kennedy Twins have written eleven other books and edited, annotated, and republished an 1825 textbook on the United States Constitution by William Rawle. The other books by the Kennedy Twins are as follows: *Why Not Freedom! America's Revolt Against Big Government, Was Jefferson Davis Right?, Reclaiming Liberty, Myths of American Slavery, Lincoln's Marxist (Donnie and Al Benson), A View of the Constitution* (William Rawle, 1825), *Nullifying Tyranny, Rekilling Lincoln, Nullification: Why and How, Uncle Seth Fought the Yankees, Punished With Poverty, Dixie Rising: Rules for Rebels,* and *Yankee Empire: Aggressive Abroad and Despotic at Home.*

Many in the media have noted the Kennedy Twins advocacy of limited government, that is, real States' Rights, which have led to several interviews and TV appearances. The Kennedy Twins have been interviewed by numerous local and national talk radio shows including Col. Oliver North's radio show, Alan Comes radio show, Bill Maher's show Politically Incorrect, BBC, and French National TV.

In 2018 the Commander-in-Chief of the Sons of Confederate Veterans (SCV) appointed Donnie Kennedy Chief of Heritage Operations and Ron Kennedy as Deputy Chief of Heritage Promotions for the SCV. Both have served as Commander of the Louisiana Division Sons of Confederate Veterans. They have received special recognition awards from the National Commander of the Sons of Confederate Veterans, the Jefferson Davis Historical Gold Medal from the United Daughters of the Confederacy and numerous other awards from various Southern Heritage organizations.

Publisher's note: Just prior to the publication of this book (July 2022), Mr. Kennedy was elected as the National Lt. Commander of the Sons of Confederate Veterans.

ADDITIONAL TITLES AVAILABLE FROM THE KENNEDYS

AND SO MUCH MORE AT SHOTWELLPUBLISHING.COM

Latest Releases & Best Sellers

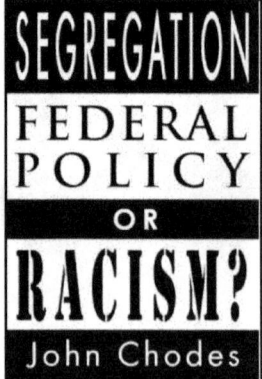

Over 70 Unapologetically Southern Titles For You To Enjoy

SHOTWELLPUBLISHING.COM

Free Book Offer

DON'T GET LEFT OUT, Y'ALL.
Sign-up and be the first to know about new releases, sales, and other goodies
—plus we'll send you TWO FREE EBOOKS!

Lies My Teacher Told Me:
The True History of the War for
Southern Independence
by Dr. Clyde N. Wilson

Confederaphobia:
An American Epidemic
by Paul C. Graham

FreeLiesBook.com

Southern Books. No Apologies.
We love the South — its history, traditions, and culture — and are proud of our inheritance as Southerners. Our books are a reflection of this love.

www.ingramcontent.com/pod-product-compliance
Lightning Source LLC
Chambersburg PA
CBHW070611170426
43200CB00012B/2651